12⁵⁰

THE ROYAL
OVER-SEAS
LEAGUE

About the author

Adele Smith has had a varied career in public relations and fund-raising. She was the Public Relations Director of the Royal Over-Seas League for four years and has maintained a strong association with the League ever since. She was born in Northumberland and educated at the Universities of Leeds and Oxford.

THE ROYAL
OVER-SEAS
LEAGUE

From Empire into Commonwealth,
A History of the First 100 Years

Adele Smith

LONDON · NEW YORK

Published in 2010 by I.B.Tauris & Co Ltd
6 Salem Road, London W2 4BU
175 Fifth Avenue, New York NY 10010
www.ibtauris.com

Distributed in the United States and Canada Exclusively
by Palgrave Macmillan
175 Fifth Avenue, New York NY 10010

Copyright © 2010 Royal Over-Seas League

The right of Adele Smith to be identified as the author of this work has been
asserted by her in accordance with the Copyright, Designs and Patents Act 1988.

All rights reserved. Except for brief quotations in a review, this book, or any
part thereof, may not be reproduced, stored in or introduced into a retrieval
system, or transmitted, in any form or by any means, electronic, mechanical,
photocopying, recording or otherwise, without the prior written permission of
the Royal Over-Seas League.

ISBN: 978 1 84885 010 1 (HB)
         978 1 84885 011 8 (PB)

A full CIP record for this book is available from the British Library
A full CIP record is available from the Library of Congress

Library of Congress Catalog Card Number: available

Typeset in Garamond by Sara Millington, Editorial and Design Services
Printed and bound in Great Britain by CPI Antony Rowe

FSC
Mixed Sources
Product group from well-managed
forests and other controlled sources
Cert no. SGS-COC-2953
www.fsc.org
© 1996 Forest Stewardship Council

We sailed wherever ship could sail,
We founded many a mighty state,
Pray God our greatness may not fail
Through craven fears of being great

Alfred Lord Tennyson

Contents

Acknowledgements

A history of this kind must necessarily be a collaborative effort. I am most grateful to all the past and present members and staff of the Royal Over-Seas League and fellow organisations who have given their time and help so generously. I am particularly indebted to Robert Newell, who has guided and overseen the whole enterprise, and to Stanley Martin, Roderick Lakin and Margaret Adrian-Vallance for their essential contributions, and to Fatima Vaniček, Samantha Whitaker and Polly Hynd for their constant help.

Two people have lent their personal archives, which have been invaluable. I am a grateful to the late Geoffrey Allen for his research papers and drawings about the Park Place buildings, and to Robin Noakes for lending the diaries and letters left to his family by his father, Philip Noakes.

I thank Viscount Norwich for permission to quote from Lady Diana Cooper's memoirs The Rainbow Comes and Goes (London: Rupert Hart-Davis, 1958) and Anne de Courcy for her recollections of her great uncle, Evelyn Wrench. Finally, I acknowledge the great help I have received from my editor, Liz Friend-Smith of I.B.Tauris, who made the entire process an enjoyable learning-curve.

Adele Smith

Illustrations

Black and white illustrations

Colour plate section (between pp.80 and 81)

This portrait of HM The Queen, by ROSL prizewinner Christian Furr, was commissioned by ROSL in 1995 and hangs in the lobby of Over-Seas House, London.

The Royal Over-Seas League was founded by Sir Evelyn Wrench in 1910, the year that my grandfather, King George V, came to the throne. Within six years, he had granted his patronage to the young society and I am delighted to have followed him and my father, King George VI, in being Patron of the League.

On its fiftieth anniversary in 1960, I was happy to approve the title 'Royal' and I have appreciated meeting its members, from the United Kingdom and the overseas Commonwealth, on many occasions during my reign.

On its centenary in 2010, I wish the Royal Over-Seas League and all its members every success for the future.

Elizabeth R

INTRODUCTION

to the History of the
Royal Over-Seas League

I n the foreword to this book, HM The Queen refers to the patronage accorded by successive monarchs to the Royal Over-Seas League almost from its inception. Under that regal umbrella, much has been achieved over the last century.

The League has never realised the rather extravagant dream of its founder, Sir Evelyn Wrench, to be an imperial society of a million members. The imagination of the young 23-year-old when he sketched out his ideas in 1906 on the trans-Canadian train *The Imperial* (*The Canadian* when my wife and I did the same journey exactly 100 years later) proved to be beyond his capacity. Yet, as Robert Browning wrote, 'Ah, but a man's reach should exceed his grasp, or what's a heaven for?'[1]

The 'heaven' that the League has achieved in reality has brought meaningful activities and companionship to many, many thousands of members over the century, as well as decisive encouragement to thousands of young musicians and artists. It has always been, as Wrench consistently urged, 'not a club, although membership includes the privileges and amenities of a club'.

I am still mildly irritated when friends sometimes enquire, 'How is the *club* doing?'

Many such friends and others refer wistfully to the days when their parents or grandparents used the clubhouse whilst on their leave from such places as India, Malaya or Africa. The passing of Empire means that the League is no longer a home in London for members of the Indian and Colonial Civil Services, although a number of members of the modern Diplomatic Service still use it when in this country. That change from a dependent Empire to an independent Commonwealth is reflected in the composition of the Central Council of the League. Its members used to include many retired Indian and colonial governors; now a number of them are retired high commissioners and ambassadors.

The League has always justified the 'Over-Seas' in its title. The old dominion and colonial shields at Over-Seas House bear witness to that. In its early days, the League spread itself throughout the world, with branches or Corresponding Secretaries in many countries, both within the Empire and outside it. Gradually, it concentrated its activities on the countries of the emerging Commonwealth and today, apart from Britain, it has branches throughout Australia, New Zealand and much of Canada. Half of its 20,000 members live outside the Britain. The competitors in its music and art competitions come from all over the Commonwealth and its charitable work is concentrated on Namibia, formerly South West Africa. It stands, four-square, as a leading loyal society of the Commonwealth.

I shall not rehearse the manifold activities over the past century that are described so carefully by Adele Smith in this knowledgeable history. Many of you will be as surprised as the Director General and I were by much of what she has uncovered and recounted – and we thought we knew a lot about the League.

I feel privileged to have been Chairman of the League since 2005, especially in the period leading to the celebration of the centenary in 2010. I have been able to help in the many preparations for that celebration, the highlight of which will be a reception at St James's Palace, graced with the presence of our Patron, HM The Queen.

No introduction by the Chairman would be complete without referring to the truly remarkable job done by Robert Newell in his 31 years of service to the League: 13 as General Manager and 18 as Director General. He has moulded the League, led its staff in raising the already high standards of service and maintained a remarkable rapport with members throughout the world. As is evident from this history, the League has been well served over the century by a number of officials, not least by a succession of chief executives. I naturally did not know the early ones but I have come to know Robert Newell very well since I joined the Central Council in 1982. The League is greatly in his debt.

The subtitle of this history is *From Empire to Commonwealth, A History of the First 100 Years* and I am sure that all who read it, whether members of the League or not, will understand the important role played by our society in that vital transition. Not many empires have been dissolved in such a relatively harmonious manner and multi-racial bodies like the League have contributed significantly to that process.

What of the future of the League? There is a tendency to think that every organisation must somehow be made 'fit for the twenty-first century' by marked change. We have grown up to think of history as being divided, somewhat artificially, into centuries. I do not believe in change purely for its own sake – 'if it ain't broke, don't fix it'. So, while the League should continue to look for new ways of its extending its work in pursuit of its basic aims – 'supporting the Commonwealth through its own social, music, arts and welfare activities' – it may well find that 'more of the same' will be a perfectly adequate objective. In any case, whatever they decide, our successors will have a very firm base on which to build during the second century of the League.

Stanley Martin, CVO
Chairman

I

Evelyn Wrench and the Founding of the Royal Over-Seas League

The Royal Over-Seas League was founded as the Over-Seas Club in 1910, at a time when the British Empire was the focus of unprecedented interest by politicians, churchmen, theorists and idealists of all kinds. The idea of Empire with its potential for the creation of an advanced multicultural society, benefiting its people both materially and spiritually, had become a dominant force in British life. Empire builders, statesmen and soldiers, such as Joseph Chamberlain, Cecil Rhodes, Dr Livingstone and General Gordon, were popular heroes.

Throughout the last two decades of the nineteenth century this interest had been building, spurred on by elements in the popular press, led by Alfred Harmsworth (Lord Northcliffe), and extending to novels and poetry, such as that of Alfred Lord Tennyson, Alfred Austin and William Henley, with particular emphasis on the excitement and adventure that the Empire seemed to offer. Periodicals for children such as *Boy's Own Paper* were full of these possibilities.[1] The new Boy Scouts organisation and sport generally prepared a boy for an adventurous life with an imperial purpose. The Boer War with its attendant atrocities caused a more sceptical mood to develop in the early 1900s, but by 1907 the imperialists were back in full force, with serious suggestions as to how the Empire could grow.

Books on Empire topics, such as *Colonial Nationalism* by Richard Jebb, and Normal Angell's *The Great Illusion*, examining the future of the imperial idea, were best-sellers.[2] This interest had led to the formation of many societies fostering Empire connections, such as the Royal Colonial Institute, the Victoria League, the Navy League and the Boy Scouts. In the Empire itself, the new countries were developing their independence and looking for ways in which they could assert their individuality without challenging their ties to the Mother Country. The first Imperial Conference was held in 1909. The question of Empire federation versus autonomy was a central theme in the years before the Great War, and politicians talked of the 'Greater Britain', seeing the Empire as integral in purpose.

At the same time, the nineteenth century had been remarkable for the growth of religious fervour and the intensity of theological dispute. Non-conformist church groups flourished, as did their missionary societies. The Oxford Movement, led by John Henry Newman, later Cardinal Newman, challenged the Church of England. Questions of doctrine existed alongside more practical expressions of Christianity, with a focus on the need to do good and to be of service to humanity at large. Earlier in the century Lord Shaftesbury had established the importance of philanthropy, and there was an increasing interest in the welfare, education and working conditions of the poor, illustrated by social studies exemplified by the work of Henry Mayhew.[3] This interest led to pressure for legislation to provide universal elementary education, the abolition of child labour in mines and factories and better working conditions for women and children in particular. The belief that mankind could be made better by a combination of religion, practical help and service to others was held increasingly by educated people at the beginning of the twentieth century.

Against this background, John Evelyn Wrench, the founder of the Over-Seas Club, later the Royal Over-Seas League, was completely a man of his time. He was born in Ireland in 1882 into an Anglo–Irish family with aristocratic connections. His boyhood at Eton was marked by illness and injury but, despite this, he emerged as a remarkably lively, mercurial personality. Leaving Eton at 17 years old, undecided whether to become a missionary or a diplomat, he travelled extensively abroad, particularly in Germany where he studied the language. With his talent for seizing opportunities, he returned to England and set up his own postcard business, modelled on the ones he had seen in Germany. The great success of this teenage venture was short-lived due to too rapid overexpansion, but his entrepreneurial skills had been noticed by Lord Northcliffe, the newspaper proprietor whose assistant and protégé he became. He worked for Amalgamated Press for eight years, editing the Over-Seas *Daily Mail* amongst other papers.

The empire-builder Cecil Rhodes had been an idol of Wrench's since boyhood, together with the whole idea of Empire brotherhood. The critical moment of Wrench's life came in 1906, when, on a visit to Ottawa, he was staying with the Governor General, Lord Grey, a Rhodes Trustee. During his visit they discussed the future of the British Empire continually, and particularly the idea of forming a great non-partisan society to promote unity throughout the Empire. Lord Grey showed Wrench a document in which Cecil Rhodes set out his ideas for just such a society to extend the influence of the Empire. During the rest of his time in Canada, Wrench formulated the idea on which the Over-Seas Club (later the ROSL) would be based. He was 23 years old at the time.

Wrench later wrote:

I left Ottawa on August 15 1906 by the train *Imperial Limited* for Winnipeg – a two day journey – and my first afternoon in the train was spent in putting down in black and white the aims and objectives of an Imperial Society such as I longed to found.

This morning Lord Grey gave me the most interesting document to look at which it has ever been my good fortune to read. It was the statement which Cecil Rhodes wrote in the year 1875, when but 22 years old, on the South African veldt … 'It often strikes a man to enquire what is the chief good in life. To one the thought comes that it is a happy marriage, to another great wealth, and as each seizes on his idea, for that he more or less works for the rest of his existence. To myself, thinking over the same question the wish came to me to render myself useful to my country.'

Surely at no time in the history of the British Empire has an equal opportunity presented itself to the practical imperialist …

In the first place, why cannot we twentieth-century British citizens put into practice the germs of the idea as it appeared to Cecil Rhodes on the South African veldt 31 years ago? There are at the present time too many organisations and leagues – take, for instance, the Royal Colonial Institute, the Victoria League, the Daughters of the Empire, the Empire League, the Empire Day Movement, the Navy League, the British-Made Goods League, and so on *ad infinitum*. What is wanted is one great Central Organisation …

The Germans, with that wonderful power of plodding, have built up a Navy League of 978,000 members, and, be it remembered, to a league which is only a copy of our own.

If we set ourselves to get a membership of 1,000,000, I believe we could do it, provided, of course, we received Royal approval, and the various societies sank their petty interests. An organisation such as I suggest – whose object would be to further the British Empire, British institutions and British liberty in every manner, would, I believe, become a tremendous power to be reckoned with …

A poor and unknown man has built the Salvation Army to its present position in some 30 years with influence, the power of the press behind him and money – we can obtain even greater results.[4]

On his return to London, Wrench worked to promote these ideas with the support (financial and otherwise) of his employer, Lord

Cecil Rhodes.

Northcliffe. At first the combination of their talents – Wrench's vision and idealism and Northcliffe's pragmatic business sense – worked harmoniously. The older man had been a father figure to Evelyn Wrench and promoted him to an important place in his newspaper empire. It was natural for Wrench to outline his vision to his chief but their interpretations of the uses to which this could be put were widely different. It was inconceivable to Northcliffe that the career path he offered could be put aside for some purely idealistic concern. When he gave support to launch the venture in the shape of the use of an office in Carmelite House, his HQ, and the publication of articles in the *Daily Mail* he was also intent on increasing circulation in the readership. Later, Evelyn Wrench reflected:

> In starting the Over-Seas Club while I was editor of the *Overseas Daily Mail* I was sowing seeds of future trouble. I was thinking solely of the welfare of the Empire. I never for a moment thought that the new movement might have a dual purpose, that of serving the Empire but also of getting circulation for the *Overseas Daily Mail*. I was quite willing for Northcliffe and the *Daily Mail* to get indirect prestige as backers of the new scheme. But the Over-Seas Club was something sacred to me.[5]

Alfred Harmsworth, Lord Northcliffe.

The 'sacred' nature of Wrench's vision for the Club is demonstrated in 'The Creed of an Imperialist', which he often quoted in his publications. Part of it reads:

I believe in our glorious Empire of Free Peoples,
In the sacredness of our mission,
In the unselfishness of our aims.
I believe in our great past
And in a greater future,
In the emptiness of riches
And the dignity of labour.

This strongly romantic side to Wrench's nature fortunately was counterbalanced by his practical working experience. Eight years spent in the hard graft of the newspaper world, involving marketing, financial affairs and networking, had helped to give him the skills needed for the successful establishment of the new enterprise.

The Launch of the Over-Seas Club

By 1910, Wrench felt that the moment had come officially to launch the new organisation. The first public meeting of the Over-Seas Club was held at the Memorial Hall, Farringdon Street, London EC on Tuesday, 27 June 1911, the week following the coronation of King George V. Over 300 members were present from all parts of the world. Great enthusiasm was shown and the future structure of the movement was discussed. Evelyn Wrench was in the Chair and among those present were Lord Northcliffe, Sir Harry Brittain, the Premier of Alberta and representatives of 62 Empire groups and interests. Initially, Wrench had planned to make membership free and just charge a shilling for the badge. It soon became apparent that this was widely believed to be a circulation gambit by Lord Northcliffe's newspapers and Wrench was forced to consider both a membership fee and his whole association with the newspapers and their proprietor.

By 1912, Wrench felt he could no longer combine his journalism with his mission and resigned from the *Daily Mail*. However, the association with Northcliffe continued for many years on a personal level, with Northcliffe designated as Founder and President of the Over-Seas Club – inviting misunderstandings both public and private as to his real role in the Club's foundation.

The same year, accompanied by his sister Winifride, Wrench undertook a 17-month, 64,000-mile tour of the Empire, which he called his 'Empire Crusade'. During this tour, entirely self-financed, he visited over 100 Club centres in Canada, Australia, New Zealand, the Union of South Africa and Rhodesia. The creation of so many branches and Honorary Corresponding Secretaries in the two years since the launch of the organisation was a remarkable achievement, and proved the popularity of the whole idea of 'Empire Brotherhood'. Public meetings were held in nearly all the important cities in the self-governing dominions. Numerous branches of the Club were formed and contacts made to secure the connections essential for its future. Evelyn Wrench himself dated the real beginning of the club from this tour.

On his return to London, Wrench found that misunderstandings still existed over the Over-Seas Club's association with the Northcliffe press, and he recognised the need to put the whole project on a proper footing. The administration to do this was accordingly established. Richard Jebb, the author of *Colonial Nationalism*[6] and a respected authority on Empire affairs, became the first Chairman of the Over-Seas Club, and a Central Council was appointed to which Evelyn Wrench, as Secretary, was responsible. The Council was composed of many distinguished people with Empire connections, and some important vice presidents were created. Enough money was quickly raised from generous donors to rent the first premises of four rooms at General Buildings, the Aldwych, opened by the Lord Mayor on Empire Day, 1914. An annual membership fee of 2*s.* 6*d.* was agreed. All this was achieved prior to the outbreak of war in August 1914.

Evelyn Wrench in his office at Over-Seas House.

Evelyn Wrench took an active part in the war, becoming a Major in the Royal Flying Corps (RFC) and working incidentally for two further newspaper proprietors in turn, in their wartime posts at the Air Board (Lord Rothermere) and the Ministry of Information (Lord Beaverbrook). Simultaneously, Wrench's work with the Over-Seas Club intensified. The Club magazine, edited by Wrench himself, was created in December 1915 and immediately became a critical arm of consolidation for members throughout the world. The tremendous fund-raising campaigns he organised among members during this period – including raising more than £1 million for comforts for the troops, providing 350 aircraft and supporting hospitals for Flying Corps Officers at the cost of £30,000 a year – proved just how strong the Empire ties had become. The Club was further strengthened by amalgamation with the Patriotic League of Britons Over-Seas in 1918, thus becoming the Over-Seas League. For his work in raising funds for the war effort, Wrench received the CMG in 1917.[7]

Nurses at the RFC Hospital supported
by the Over-Seas Club, 1915.

RFC pilots recuperating at the hospital.

Certificate awarded to children in Christmas 1915 who supported the Over-Seas Club fund-raising for the troops.

When asked to describe the organisation he had created, Evelyn Wrench liked to quote Lord Baden Powell's description: 'The Over-Seas League is for grown-ups, and Boy Scouts for the growing-ups', or, more simply, 'Scouts are for boys, the Over-Seas League is for grown-ups'. At the end of the war, Evelyn Wrench envisaged that the huge numerical success of the Scouting movement world-wide would be repeated in the Over-Seas League.

In 1918 Evelyn Wrench also founded the English Speaking Union, a new organisation to promote friendship between the Empire and the USA, believing that close cooperation between the two great English-speaking powers would be important in the post-war period.

By 1922, Evelyn Wrench had joined the Board of the periodical the *Spectator* and he bought a controlling interest in the paper, serving as Editor from 1925–32. He later sold his interest to Ian Gilmour MP, but he remained Chairman of the Board for the rest of his life. Travel writer Peter Fleming was working for the *Spectator* at the time and recorded his impression of Evelyn Wrench as being 'benignly handsome, outwardly naive, with a high-pitched voice and a rather fluttery manner … behind his gentle façade … lay a streak of canny toughness'.[8]

Wrench always believed in the Empire as a free and equal association of peoples, non-racist and democratic. An early proponent of self-government for all colonies, he claimed that his first Empire tour in 1912 had made him see all future UK–Empire questions through Empire eyes. He also learnt from his work during the first war, recruiting in the large impoverished cities of Great Britain, how bad conditions were for the majority of people, and his desire to give them a better chance in the Empire later led to more controversial projects in the post-war period. His energy and idealism had given the League its character and success: 'What others have dreamed, you have done.'[9] His practical organisational skills drove it forward.

First Welfare Project of the Over-Seas Club:

Sir Frederick Truby King and the Babies of the Empire

A crusade for the health of women and children for the honour of the Empire, under the auspices of the Over-Seas Club.

Launched in 1917, and described by Evelyn Wrench as 'the first important piece of social work with which we identified ourselves', this crusade had its origins in the first world tour undertaken by Evelyn Wrench and his sister Winifride in 1912. They arrived in New Zealand with introductions to leading New Zealand politicians and influential people, including the Premier W.F. Massey and Dr Truby King, a famous medical pioneer, whose work with children was of particular interest to Winifride Wrench since she intended to make a career in infant welfare on her return to England.

Truby King had originally been in charge of a large government hospital for mental diseases in Ortagao, which had the benefit of an adjoining 1,000-acre farm. He began to study the animals and apply his theories of rearing young animals in as natural an environment as possible with proper ventilation and natural food. The marked improvement in their health, weight and resistance to disease gave him the idea of launching a parallel project to introduce a more natural environment for human infants, together with a sensible education for their mothers in child-rearing. Supported by Lady Plunket, the wife of the Governor General, in 1907 Truby King founded the Plunket Society for the Promotion of the Health of Women and Children, where the first Plunket nurse was trained and appointed to teach mothers healthier methods of child-rearing. There was an immediate and positive response to this initiative. At that time the infant mortality rate in New Zealand was 2,000 per 25,000 babies. As a result of Dr King's work, within five years this had been halved. His fame spread rapidly.

On her return from the world tour Winifride Wrench resumed her work with child welfare and with Lady Plunket, now resident in England, formed the ambition of inviting Truby King to England to launch a similar crusade to the one which had been so successful in

New Zealand. Despite the war, late in 1917 this project was realised, sponsored by the Over-Seas Club. The New Zealand Government agreed to lend the services of Dr King to the Club for a six-month period to launch 'The Babies of the Empire Training Centre' in Trebour Road, London. Financial support came from the members of the Club worldwide. Public opinion at this stage of a war notable for terrible loss of life was ready to support an effort to save and improve the lives of a new generation. Medical opinion, too, had been carefully cultivated to support the plan by eminent doctors such as Lord Dawson of Penn. A committee was formed to oversee the new movement, with medical direction passing to St Thomas' Hospital. In 1925 Cromwell House in Highgate was bought to house the newly named 'Mothercare and Training Centre', and Winifride Wrench's interest in the project continued.

The purposes of the project were to prepare women mentally and physically for childbirth; and to encourage breast feeding and natural health and hygiene; to acquire and disseminate information on all matters relating to the health of women and children via demonstrations, lectures, books and articles and particularly through the training of qualified nurses to undertake these tasks. Dr King defined his approach to the whole welfare project as 'common sense, scientifically applied'.

The Overseas Aircraft Flotilla

In the autumn of 1914 Evelyn Wrench considered the part that the Over-Seas Club could play in supporting the war effort. He decided to organise an 'Overseas Aircraft Flotilla' by asking members in each part of the Empire to subscribe for an aeroplane to be presented to the RFC, and named after the district which provided it. Although he recalled that he had never seen an aircraft of any sort during his 64,000-mile tour of the Empire, he recognised their future importance in the war, and the way in which, for a comparatively small sum, Over-Seas Club members in each district could make a personal contribution to the war effort. He wrote to the Army Council in January 1915 asking for permission to start the project, which was immediately granted.

Queen Alexandra with RFC pilots of the Over-Seas aeroplanes.

An aeroplane donated by Over-Seas Club members during the First World War.

The two aeroplanes used by the RFC at this time were the 100 HP Gnome, Vickers Gun Bi-plane, complete with gun, costing £2,250, and the 70 HP Renault BE ZC, costing £1,500. Within four months, six aircraft had been presented, prompting letters of appreciation from the King and Lord Kitchener. Acting on the publicity this provided, Evelyn Wrench had 100,000 leaflets printed for distribution throughout the Empire. The enormous response that followed (£100,000 in the first year) continued throughout the war, with some areas contributing through the fund and others directly. The Patriotic League of Britons Overseas, later to be amalgamated with the Over-Seas Club, had meanwhile sponsored 50 seaplanes and aeroplanes independently.

Altogether, as a result of the propaganda initiated by Evelyn Wrench, some 350 aeroplanes had been presented by 1918, 172 directly at a cost of £278,250, named for their district (Victoria, Nova Scotia, Hong Kong) or more creatively (The Springbok, A Devil Bird from Ceylon). If the original machines were destroyed the RFC arranged for others to be named after them, continuing the link. Queen Alexandra was the very active patron of the fund, visiting the Flying Corps pilots in training with the Over-Seas Club planes.

II

Development of the League

The Over-Seas League had emerged from the Great War with its imperial connections greatly strengthened. The immense fund-raising efforts organised so admirably by Evelyn Wrench and Lady des Voeux, his cousin and Director of Correspondence, had drawn attention to the League from many important quarters, and internally the support of the overseas and home branches had shown that the ideals of the original club could be practically fulfilled in a way unimaginable before 1914.

Nevertheless, the post-war period was a difficult time financially, and it is much to the credit of the Patriotic League of Britons Overseas and the Over-Seas Club that, by 1922, the character of the combined organisations had emerged successfully. With the granting of the Royal Charter in that year, the objectives of the Over-Seas League were established. Principal amongst these were:

- to draw together in the bond of comradeship British citizens throughout the world;
- to render individual service to the British Commonwealth of Nations;

- to maintain the power of the British Commonwealth of Nations and to hold to its best traditions; and
- to help one another.

An organisation with such ideals was bound to be democratic in practice. Despite the insistence in all early magazines that the League was 'not a club' but a worldwide League of Friendship, once premises were established in St James's the unusual character of the membership must have been striking in the heart of London's club land. From the beginning no distinction was made on grounds of race, creed or gender among the membership. At that time a club in St James's that welcomed women on an equal footing was unique and did much to determine the future independent character of the League.

The Prince of Wales with Lady des Voeux and Sir Ernest Birch
at the opening of the new premises 1922.

The President and Central Council appointed Lady des Voeux, Director of Correspondence, to be Controller, effectively in charge of all administration at Over-Seas House, an honorary post that she held for over 20 years. Evelyn Wrench himself combined the roles of Executive Director with the editorship of the journal. As usual he was constantly making new contacts and alliances for the League. A formidable list of Vice Presidents was established, including the Duke of Devonshire, the Rt Hon. David Lloyd George, the Marquess Curzon of Kedleston, the Rt Hon. Winston Churchill, Lord Leverhulme, Viscount Milner and Lord Baden Powell. A new Travelling Secretary and the greatly enlarged magazine both helped to maintain the momentum of the war years. Membership stood at 27,000 at this time. There were many branches and 800 Honorary Corresponding Secretaries around the world. The immediate target for membership was 50,000.

Expansion of the Club Premises

To match these ambitions the Club had to expand physically. The first premises of four rooms in the Aldwych were quickly outgrown. By 1916, at the height of the First World War, it was decided that, as a fitting tribute to the contribution made by the Empire to the war effort, a building fund should be launched. A new building would serve as a permanent War Memorial. Although the main fund-raising efforts were devoted to comforts for the troops, hospitals and aircraft, the idea was established and the War Memorial Fund began. In 1919, talks about a possible amalgamation with another Empire Society, the Royal Commonwealth, and the purchase of a building adjoining their premises in Northumberland Avenue, failed. The search for suitable premises became urgent.

In 1921, appropriately enough on Empire Day, Evelyn Wrench visited Vernon House in Park Place, St James's, SW1, for the first time. Put on the market by Lady Hillingdon for £45,000, the house was bought by the League with money from the building fund. A tablet by the doorway of the new Over-Seas House confirmed this as the League's War Memorial. Over the next few years the lease of number 3 and the freeholds of 4 and 5 Park Place were added to provide offices and a Club House with a bar and bedrooms for male members. By 1934, when space was again becoming a problem, Rutland House next door was bought from the Dowager Duchess of Rutland, with the necessary £73,000 purchase price again being raised by an appeal to the membership. The addition of the Westminster Wing in 1937 completed the nucleus of buildings referred to by Evelyn Wrench as his 'Empire Centre'. The increased space in the newly acquired buildings provided not only better facilities, bedrooms and dining rooms but also conference rooms and an Empire newspaper room.

Evelyn Wrench's paternalistic presence decided the League's development. During the 1920s and 1930s he divided his time mainly between the Over-Seas League and the English Speaking Union, both of which prospered. His diaries reveal the extraordinary amount of work, travel, speeches and connections he undertook. He had great charm and skill in organisation. Some of his ideas failed to prosper, for instance, an attempt to found an Irish Unity League during the First World War, and later an All People's Association to promote Anglo–German understanding in the 1930s. However, he always remained open to new ideas and concepts and was adept at finding ways to implement them.

From the first the League was to be an organisation with a double purpose – welcoming travellers to the UK, making them feel at home and solving their problems, but also sending advice, information and, in some cases, people out to the Empire. The administration in the 1920s and 1930s was organised to reflect all these needs.

Evelyn Wrench's Bentley

In 1927 one of the oldest League members, Stuart Elliott, wrote to the Chairman of the Central Council, Sir Ernest Birch, suggesting that a presentation should be made to Evelyn Wrench to recognise all his great work on behalf of the Empire. The Chairman accordingly contacted all members of the League through the magazine, with the help of Lady des Voeux, in July 1927. He wrote, 'With so large a membership as ours I hope that it will be easy to present Mr Wrench with a motor car. Donations need not be large...'

An article in *Overseas* earlier in the year by Evelyn Wrench himself asking the question 'What is my new car to be?' may have suggested the appropriate nature of the gift. The Chairman was quite right to be optimistic: 1,600 members subscribed and a 4.5 litre Bentley was bought and presented, resplendent in black and red.

Evelyn Wrench with the Bentley presented to him by members in 1927.

Banquet at the Royal Albert Hall to celebrate the League's 21st birthday, 2 July 1931.

A Banquet at the Royal Albert Hall to Celebrate the Over-Seas League's 21st Birthday

On 2 July 1931 a banquet was held for League members at the Royal Albert Hall to mark the 21 years since the foundation of the Over-Seas League. Most of the lower tiers and boxes were filled and approximately 1,000 members out of a total of 45,000 attended. As a special distinction, HRH Edward, Prince of Wales, Vice-Patron, attended and proposed the health of the League. Philip Snowden, Secretary of State for the Dominions proposed the Loyal Toast.

Music on appropriate Dominion themes was performed by the band of the Royal Horse Guards (the Blues) with an organ solo of 'Homage to the Father', and pipe music was provided by the Gaelic Society Pipers for the London Scottish Reel Team.

When Evelyn Wrench wrote a treatise in 1935 describing the 'Empire Centre' and its purposes, an information/over-seas service bureau, travel bureau, trade intelligence, Empire fellowship, British National Union, migration bureau and reception centre providing help with accommodation were all flourishing. The needs of two of Evelyn Wrench's many initiatives with other societies were mentioned specifically: the alliance with the Red Cross, dating from 1914, a detachment described as 'one of the best in London', and, more controversially to modern thinking, the Empire migration and 'Back to the Land Scheme'. The migration initiatives had begun after the war to help discharged servicemen wanting to start a new life in Canada. They developed in idealistic fashion in this period to help poor children to have a new life in the Empire under the auspices of the New Zealand Government, the YMCA and the Fairbridge Society, or in Great Britain with the Back to the Land Scheme, which helped teenagers to find jobs on British farms.

The
OVER-SEAS LEAGUE

{Incorporated by Royal Charter}
PATRON: HIS MAJESTY THE KING

THE OVER-SEAS LEAGUE is a non-party society formed to promote the unity of British subjects in all parts of the World.

ITS FOUR CHIEF OBJECTS ARE:

1. To draw together in the bond of comradeship British subjects the world over.
2. To render individual service to the Empire.
3. To maintain the power of the Empire and to hold to its best traditions.
4. To help one another.

MEMBERS' CREED

Believing the British Empire to stand for justice, freedom, order and good government, we pledge ourselves, as citizens of the British Commonwealth of Nations, to maintain the heritage handed down to us by our fathers.

THIS IS TO WITNESS THAT

was duly enrolled as a member of the Over-Seas League in

on 19

World Headquarters
Vernon House
London S.W. 1

Secretary

New design for the membership certificate in 1934.

Many League branches raised funds enthusiastically to support children in these projects, believing that in a period of depression at home a much better future could be found for them in the Empire. However good the intentions, and fortunate as the outcome was for many, the system relied on the absolute integrity of the people involved in its administration, and it seems completely unacceptable to us today that the fate of children's lives should have been decided in this way. The alliance with one or other organisation involved continued until the 1950s when League sponsorship and practical help for families wishing to emigrate to Australia took its place.

Connections with other projects proved much happier. The ROSL had a long association with the excellent Ranfurly Library Service, allowing for the dispatch of much needed books to the overseas Commonwealth. Similarly, after the Second World War all members of Voluntary Service Overseas were entitled to honorary membership of the League for one year.

Over-Seas House was widely used by members for entertainment, meetings and to establish societies, many of which survive today. The Discussion Circle, London Group, and music and educational initiatives such as debating competitions, all reflected the interests of the League. A tradition began of giving temporary membership to visiting groups from overseas such as cadets and students, and private hospitality was always offered by home members. Chairmen's lunches, Lady des Voeux's receptions and visits to events of the season, including House of Commons teas, were popular. Voluntary hostesses were on duty daily to provide practical information and help to visiting members.

Evelyn Wrench, knighted in 1932, married his widowed cousin, Lady des Voeux in 1937, cementing a partnership that had already given him great support in his enterprises, particularly at the ROSL. He had admired her and depended on her judgement since childhood. Indeed, he remained close to all his family, particularly to his mother and his powerful sister Winifride. She had accompanied him on his tours abroad and played a part in developing membership of the League, particularly in Scotland.

The wedding of Sir Evelyn Wrench and Lady des Voeux in 1937.

In 1940 Sir Evelyn and Lady Wrench embarked on a tour of North America, Singapore and India, becoming stranded in India as the events of the war caught up with them. Sir Evelyn quickly familiarised himself with the situation and was appointed by the Viceroy to the post of American Relations Officer with the government of India. He subsequently wrote a book about this period of his life called *Immortal Years*.[1] Necessarily his association with the League became more remote, with the day-to-day control passing to others. Wrench received many honours including the KCMG[2] on the 50th anniversary of the foundation of the ROSL. He devoted his later life to writing biographies, notably one of Lord Milner, as well as his memoirs. He died in 1966.

The Second World War saw the League become a centre for hospitality for servicemen of all ranks and nationalities. As in 1914, funds were raised on a large scale to provide comforts, tobacco and gifts for the troops, but now there was a large building to offer constant hospitality, all organised by the powerful Allies Welcome Committee (1940–50) under the chairmanship of Sir Jocelyn Lucas.

The Allies Welcome Committee 1940–50

The first Canadian troops coming to Britain to fight in the war arrived on 11 December 1939. The various Empire societies began immediately to organise hospitality for them and for the large number of Empire servicemen who followed. It was soon realised that no similar provision had been made for the great influx of allied forces from occupied nations – French, Dutch, Belgian, Norwegian, Polish and Czech – who, together with their exiled governments, found refuge in the UK.

At the Over-Seas League, Sir Jocelyn Lucas, MC, was already Head of Hospitality. This remarkable man, MP for Portsmouth South from 1939 to 1966, combined his activities with the Club with parliamentary duties and arduous part-time work as an auxiliary fireman. Since the rules of the Over-Seas Club originally precluded raising money for anything but Commonwealth causes, he realised the need to form an independent Allies Welcome Committee to extend hospitality to all troops regardless of race, nationality, rank or gender. As Chairman, backed by an influential committee, he raised money to support hospitality not only from members but also from wealthy individuals and large businesses. The Committee started its work in 1940, soon after Dunkirk. The first dinner was given in August of that year for the Free French Officers and members of the French government who had escaped to London. This was followed by a weekly luncheon for each ally and Dominion in turn, and for the American Eagle Squadron.

Despite wartime shortages, bombings and the diminished staff at Over-Seas House, and with meals sometimes cooked over oil stoves when air raids cut off gas supplies, from the first these lunches were a great success, enabling guests to meet their British opposite numbers. Photographs of these events were forbidden in case of enemy reprisals on relatives who remained in occupied Europe.

With the lunches established, the Committee began a series of receptions to bring the Allied Forces themselves together. They were held on the first Tuesday of every month throughout the war, regardless of air raids, V1s or V2s. Quite quickly the numbers attending rose to several hundred, beyond the capacity of Over-Seas House, and the receptions had to be transferred to the Dorchester Hotel.

Two of these occasions were particularly memorable. The first was held by chance on D-Day when the guest of honour was Mr Winant, the American ambassador. The French generals Le Clerc and Koenig were also present. The second time was during the week of the Victory Parade when representatives from every detachment taking part were invited.

The Committee entertained nearly every war leader present in London at that time, with General de Gaulle being one of the first. Royal guests included HMs the Kings of Greece and Yugoslavia, the Crown Prince of Norway, Prince Bernhard of the Netherlands, the Princess Royal, the Duchess of Kent and the Duke of Gloucester. Guests also included heads of the British forces such as Lord Fraser and Sir John Cunningham from the Navy, Field Marshals Lord Alexander, Sir William Slim, Lord Wilson and Viscount Wavell from the Army, and Lords Trenchard, Tedder and Portal from the Air Force.

*Admiral of the Fleet Sir John Cunningham and Admiral
Earl Mountbatten of Burma, with Indian guests.*

HRH the Princess Royal with, left to right:
Lt JWK Champ, of Geelong, Victoria, Australia, Lt JG Rawson, of
Victoria, Australia, and Lt G Bolding, of Morewell, Victoria, Australia.

Viscount Wavell with a Soviet soldier.

Much hospitality was less formal. Parties of all kinds were popular, from fork lunches and tea parties and broadcasts to dances held several times a week, which drew large crowds. Sir Jocelyn Lucas estimated that on average 3,000 servicemen and women passed through Over-Seas House each week. A dedicated group of volunteers ran all the activities. Out in the rest of the UK the League's branches were also very active, particularly in Liverpool, Ulster, Edinburgh, Glasgow and Cardiff, where large groups of servicemen were made welcome both at the club's premises and in private homes. Private hospitality indeed was extensive, especially at Christmas time, and this tremendous effort by League members was paralleled by fund-raising activities to provide comfort for the troops abroad and help at home for sufferers of the effects of war.

In 1950, with the war safely over, the Committee was wound up. Sir Jocelyn, who had also been Chairman of the returned Prisoner of War Advice Committee, wrote: 'The term Allies infers war. We wish to remember old friends but to forget past differences and we feel therefore, that the time has come to cease our activities.'[3] The officers of the Committee in May 1950 were: President – Rt Hon. Anthony Eden MP; Vice Presidents Marie Marchioness of Willingdon and the Countess Mountbatten of Burma; and Founder and Chairman Sir Jocelyn Lucas.

All this despite wartime shortages and severe bomb damage to Vernon House in April 1941, when a direct hit burnt out rooms on the upper floors, destroying bedrooms, offices and most of the archives. In the difficult period after the war, the overseas members sent parcels of clothing and food to help distressed Londoners.

With Evelyn Wrench working in India during this period, the Assistant Secretary, Eric Rice, assumed responsibility as Secretary. His long service with the League (he had only had one other job) was typical of the careers of many of the staff who gave years of loyal service. Eric Rice finally retired in 1946. He was succeeded by Air Vice-Marshal Malcolm Henderson, as Director General.

The Director General Philip Crawshaw (front centre, with Denis Cramer on his right) with delegates to the Twentieth-Century Group World Conference in the 1950s.

Philip Crawshaw, another long-serving and well-loved member of staff, became Secretary General in 1956 and, from 1959 to 1979, Director General. This was a difficult period for the League, but nevertheless Over-Seas House continued to host many groups of visitors and events. Particularly prominent at this time was the Twentieth-Century Group for young members, founded by Florence Norden in 1936, suspended during the war and returning successfully after 1946 with up to 3,000 members at one time, under the patronage of Princess Alexandra and the Hon. Angus Ogilvy. The group organised wide-ranging activities both at home and abroad, and an annual conference of members worldwide was held at Over-Seas House between 1951 and 1962. This was also a period of much activity in the fields of the arts and education, with many

Earl Mountbatten shows the League's new Royal Charter with
the help of Bluemantle Pursuivant of the College of Arms.

student visitors. Regular broadcasts by the BBC of programmes
from St Andrew's Hall included the People and Politics series. The
League's Golden Jubilee in 1960 was celebrated with a visit by The
Queen and the granting of the official title 'Royal', together with a
coat of arms. In 1962 membership reached 50,933, of which 9,000
were life members. Following the death of Sir Evelyn Wrench in
1966, a memorial fund to sponsor music and art was launched in
his memory.

The period of high inflation that followed found the Loyal Societies of the Commonwealth – the Royal Commonwealth Society,

the Victoria League, the Royal Over-Seas League and the English Speaking Union – in financial difficulties. Currency regulations in some Commonwealth countries made payment for membership difficult, and indeed membership generally declined. Not for the first time, the idea of a merger between organisations with so many shared interests appeared attractive. A committee under Sir Anthony Burney, the chairman of Debenhams, was set up in 1980 to examine the possibilities. The initial proposal was to try to combine the first three societies on one site (the English Speaking Union having made progress independently). One idea, that all premises should be sold and the money used to establish a large Commonwealth Centre in London, proved to be impossibly expensive. An alternative idea, that the three societies should combine on either the RCS site in Northumberland Avenue or on the ROSL site in Park Place, turned out to be equally difficult. No one site could provide the requisite bedroom and office accommodation and there were further difficulties relating to individual status and debts. After protracted negotiations no satisfactory solution could be found. In the event all the Loyal Societies resolved their difficulties and continued to operate independently.

In the case of the ROSL a turning point in the League's affairs was reached in the early 1980s when the Central Council, under the direction of Lord Grey of Naunton and Sir David Scott and with a new Director General, Captain John Rumble RN (rtd), and a new and enterprising General Manager, Robert Newell, transformed the League's fortunes by selling property in Park Place. The sum raised cancelled the League's debts and enabled a complete renovation of the premises to take place.

In a period when clubs in London were amalgamating or closing, the ROSL was able to compete with hotels and professional premises whilst maintaining the strong Commonwealth connections so essential to its character. A greater emphasis on conference use and the creation of corporate membership made the ROSL popular with people who had not considered club membership

Over-Seas House and the old Park Place buildings before their
demolition in the 1980s.

before. The membership records themselves were overhauled and
computerised, which gave a more accurate picture of the subscrip-
tion base. The active exchange with reciprocal clubs throughout the
world continued and after 1998 the Central Council voted to extend
membership to non-Commonwealth citizens.

The traditional societies continue to meet at Over-Seas House
and the Discussion Group, formally the Discussion Circle, meets
regularly. The group has maintained a very high profile over the
years with meetings open to all members and their guests and a
programme of excellent speakers. The London Group with its own
membership combines monthly meetings with visits to places of
interest throughout the year. In addition there is a full events programme organised by the Public Relations Department with limited

Inter-Club reception for younger members at the
Royal Over-Seas League.

The Public Relations Department organise a full programme for the season:
Dr Chris Nonis (far left), ROSL representative Sri Lanka and Chairman,
Mackwood Tea Company, and his management team with
Mr Stanley Martin, the Chairman, on the House of Commons
Terrace at the ROSL members' tea in 2006.

tickets for events such as Wimbledon and Trooping the Colour. A long tradition of teas at the House of Commons has been kindly hosted by Members of Parliament, and recently at the House of Lords, by the President of the ROSL, Lord Luce. There is a welcome renewal and regeneration of the Younger Members Group as the Inter-Club Group combining with younger members from other clubs to offer balls, drinks parties and visits, much like the Twentieth-Century Group in its heyday. ROSL ARTS continues to attract particular interest both in the UK and overseas.

In addition to the ROSL's own societies, some groups have used the Club for regular meetings for many years, making it in fact their home. A good example of this is the Cricket Society, founded independently in 1945 as the Cricket Statistical Society, which first used the old League premises in 3 Park Place to house their cricket library in what was the Men's Reading Room, and to hold meetings there. When these premises were demolished the library and their meetings transferred to Over-Seas House, with handsome bookcases being built to house the library on the second and third floors of the Westminster Wing. Some Cricket Society members are members of the League and all regard Over-Seas House as their base.

The League has the satisfaction of knowing that professional standards have been achieved and maintained at the Club over many decades without the loss of the personal element so distinctive to the ROSL – a difficult balance critical to its success.

III

The Royal Connection

One of Evelyn Wrench's most significant early achievements was securing the patronage of the King for the newly established Over-Seas Club. Within six years of its foundation, in 1916, King George V had agreed to become patron and he continued in this role until his death in 1936. This was more than a nominal interest; records show an active exchange of letters with the Palace, particularly between 1916 and 1918 when the King's private secretary wrote frequently to congratulate the Club on its wartime fund-raising efforts to provide aeroplanes and comforts for the troops. Indeed, the King started the Over-Seas Club's fifth war fund ('They've Remembered Us') with a personal gift of £25.

Royal patronage, once established, has continued under every subsequent monarch: Edward VIII (1936), George VI (1936–52) and Queen Elizabeth II (1952 to the present day). In addition there was an early tradition of other members of the royal family becoming vice-patrons and, later, presidents of the ROSL. Prince Arthur, Duke of Connaught, Queen Victoria's youngest son, was a vice-patron from 1916 to 1942 and Edward, Prince of Wales, was also a vice-patron from 1922 until his accession in 1936. All four of

George V's surviving sons were involved with the League in the 1920s and 1930s; Albert, Duke of York, was a very active president from 1922 and George, Duke of Kent, followed his brother in this role. Henry, Duke of Gloucester, was a vice-patron from 1942 to 1974. It is unimaginable today, in an era of intense royal engagements, that so many members of the royal family should be involved simultaneously with one organisation.

The granting of a Royal Charter to the League in 1922 was of course an important step in establishing the connection. In the early years, royal visits to Over-Seas House were invariably made to mark advances in the League's life, usually the opening of further premises on the site in Park Place.

These ceremonial occasions, though important, were perhaps not as significant as the visit of King George and Queen Mary in 1922 to mark their appreciation of the active role the League had played in raising more than £1 million (approximately £50 million in today's terms) towards the war effort between 1914 and 1918. A similar visit after the Second World War by King George VI and Queen Elizabeth, accompanied by Princess Elizabeth and Princess Margaret, took place on 28 May 1946. Hundreds of Commonwealth servicemen and women gathered in St Andrew's Hall to welcome the royal party who paid tribute to the part played by the whole Empire in the war effort. Early in the war, in 1940, Queen Elizabeth had made a visit to meet many of the servicemen who had been evacuated from Dunkirk. Other members of the royal family were frequent visitors during the Second World War joining Allied Forces invited to receptions at the club.

The League did not become officially 'Royal' until 1960 when, to mark the 50th anniversary, The Queen graciously conferred the designation and made a visit, accompanied by the Duke of Edinburgh. It was appropriate that Sir Evelyn Wrench lived to see the title given to the organisation to which he had devoted so much of his life. The Queen also came to Over-Seas House on the League's 60th anniversary in 1970 and again in 1980 and 1990.

King George V and Queen Mary visit Over-Seas House in 1922.

The then Duchess of York, later Queen Elizabeth, at the
Over-Seas League garden party in Regent's Park in 1923.

King George VI (as Duke of York) signing the League Silver Jubliee Book.

King George VI and Queen Elizabeth talk to servicewomen during their visit to the League in 1946.

Other members of the royal family have played a significant part in the life of the League. Princess Alexandra, cousin of The Queen, has been a vice-patron of the ROSL for more than 25 years. Initially connected with the 20th Century (Young Members) Group, her very active interest in the Music Competition has continued over the years, both in attendance at the final concert and in encouraging young musicians, on occasion giving the prizes, and also enabling concerts to take place at St James's Palace under her patronage.

Earl Mountbatten of Burma, the last royal member to be president (1942–79), was much involved in League events both at home and abroad, particularly during and immediately after the war when Countess Mountbatten joined him in hosting occasions for Commonwealth and Allied troops. Lord Mountbatten became Grand President in 1959. His daughter, now Countess Mountbatten, a vice-president, has continued this interest, opening the most recent extensions to the west wing in 1987 and 2004.

HM The Queen at Over-Seas House to mark the 80th anniversary
of the League in 1990.

The Director General, Robert Newell, with the Earl of Wessex at a celebration
to mark The Queen's Golden Jubilee in Kenya in 2002 at the Nairobi Club.

Visits to Over-Seas House are, of course, the most obvious sign of the royal connection. However, from the 1920s onwards many League events have taken place throughout the Commonwealth which have had the distinction of a royal presence. In 1923 alone the Duke and Duchess of York attended a League garden party in the Botanic Gardens, Regent's Park, and later in the year the Prince of Wales attended a Dominion banquet at the Ritz Hotel organised by the ROSL. Recent years have seen many visits by The Queen, the Duke of Edinburgh and their family to Commonwealth countries where League members were invited to be present at welcoming receptions. The League receives recognition for the connection in other ways – through regular invitations to Royal Garden Parties for members, and the privilege of attending Promenade Concerts in The Queen's box, for example.

Perhaps, more importantly, to mark the connection in a modern and relevant way, the ROSL is now accredited as an official Civil Society Organisation of the Commonwealth. This means that since 1991 a League representative has frequently been present at Commonwealth meetings where the heads of government assemble after an opening ceremony by The Queen. Sir Evelyn Wrench would have recognised this involvement with the widest possible aspects of the Commonwealth as a great achievement and proof that the ROSL is constant in its ideals and practical in their application.

Communications

Overseas Magazine

I t was not surprising that Evelyn Wrench, trained as a newspaper man, was determined to establish a journal for the new society as soon as possible. Despite the difficulties and paper shortages of wartime Britain he launched *Overseas*, a monthly magazine for members, edited by himself, in December 1915. Early contributors included George Bernard Shaw, A.A. Milne and Harry Lauder. King George V, the Prince of Wales and the Prime Ministers H.H. Asquith and Lloyd George were among the many distinguished and busy people who sent personal messages to the magazine, acknowledging the great contribution made by members of the Over-Seas Club to the war effort.

Evelyn Wrench's view of what the magazine could achieve was ambitious from the beginning: 'My vision of *Overseas* was a journal dedicated to the highest ideals, which would ultimately earn for itself a unique place in the literature of the Empire.'[1] He later claimed it was 'The Foundation on which our edifice rests'.[2]

The first edition of *Overseas* comprised 32 pages including eight pages of advertising, taken only from British firms. There was a strict embargo on advertisements for alcohol. With a cover by the popular artist Macdonald Gill, its identity was established quickly. The cost of the first four years of production (£1,000 a year) was paid for by Alec Cochrane, an American and early Wrench supporter. The magazine was intended to be a 'non-political', positive arm of Empire, to offset German propaganda. The Empire War Aims were set out and social questions discussed ranged from housing, slums and public ownership of the drink trade to garden cities and the decimal system. A special 'Khaki' supplement was provided for the troops monthly and an armistice special issue reflected how London welcomed the peace.

In 1922 there was a great increase in the length of the journal. Regular features now included Evelyn Wrench's monthly newsletter, which was extensive and rambling, covering topics of the moment, political situations at home and overseas, details of his travels and general philosophy. There were reviews of new books and London theatre productions, 'Sport at home and overseas' (including football results!), a motoring column and a series 'Why I went overseas and what happened to me', as well as articles on every imaginable Empire topic. Large numbers of photographs enlivened the text.

Overseas was used as the main tool in the League's many fund-raising efforts, starting from the earliest editions. Articles exhorting members to greater efforts and the publication of lists of contributors' names and gifts encouraged fund-raising in wartime and beyond. The detailed accounts printed for the campaign to buy Rutland House took up pages of the journal, for example, but were remarkably effective.

As early as 1917 a special column for female readers was established, with the Editor noting, 'we have now such a large number of women members that we feel they will appreciate a monthly letter'. This was 'From a woman's standpoint', written anonymously under the nom de plume 'Wayfarer'. The variety of information and comment was extensive, with one of the first articles in 1917 featuring 'The most interesting post held by a woman in England!'.

This was Lloyd George's (the Prime Minister's) Secretary, 'Fair and attractive, 26-year-old Frances Stevenson', who went on to play a more influential role in his life, eventually becoming the second Lady Lloyd George.

New jobs for women were featured frequently – including women preachers, police officers and munitions workers during the Second World War – as was, of course, the whole issue of girls' education. The journal made a consistent attempt, begun in 1917 and continuing until at least 1945, to relate women to the modern world.

Health and exercise featured, too, with articles such as 'Exercises for women who do their own housework' and 'The future of the figure from the health and beauty point of view' reflecting the increasing awareness of health issues in the 1930s. The League's connection with the Mothercare and Training Centre, established by Dr Trudy King and Winifride Wrench (see Chapter I), continued with a Mothercraft Column with advice for mothers from Miss Liddiard, the director.

Advertising grew rapidly, with an emphasis on charities: Dr Barnado's, the National Children's Adoption Association and Ladies in Reduced Circumstances, plus practical suggestions for overseas visitors concerning car hire, hotels and other services. From the 1930s onwards health charities were more prominent, with cancer and tuberculosis charities advertising regularly, whilst simultaneously cigarettes such as Craven A., Balkan Sobranie and Rothmans were advertised monthly. There were also many personal advertisements. After 1945, reduced space severely limited the advertising copy, and there was a shift in emphasis towards travel overseas, reflecting a move from the UK to wider horizons rather than the other way round. Charities and private services continued to feature.

The more pronounced political character of the earlier magazines is exemplified in the regular Cartoons of the Month, reprinted from other publications, sometimes foreign. Other domestic cartoons also featured.

Continued on page 60...

'From a woman's standpoint', Jan. 1926 (an extract).

FROM A WOMAN'S STANDPOINT

NEW YEAR THOUGHTS

Another Christmas has come and gone and December, the greatest selling and giving month of the year, has passed on its way, and January and a new year lies stretched out before us.

We are tempted to let speculation run riot in our minds. What secrets does 1926 hold within its breast? What joys, what sorrows for you and me, for our country and for the world? At any rate, there is a greater spirit of good-will abroad than there has been since the outbreak of the World War, and we can only hope and pray that, as the weeks and months pass, the spirit of the Locarno Pact will enter more deeply into the lives of us all, and that, indeed, would mean a happy New Year to the majority of dwellers in the Western World … As each year passes, we are slowly, painfully slowly, becoming a healthier race. For another, we are slowly, again painfully slowly, becoming a more humane people.

We treat our prisoners far better than we did, even twenty-five years ago. Before long the same progress will be found in our treatment of the inmates of our lunatic asylums.

And women, who in the last resort are the supreme civilisers of the world, they too will be surer of themselves sure of their task of asserting Life as triumphant always and everywhere over form and mechanism … it is for women to be awake in all these matters, and to lead man as she never has done, through love to those higher heights that lie far off on the horizon, of which we catch but a glimpse to-day.

SHOPPING INTELLIGENTLY

Allow your thoughts to ponder for one minute on what the world would be like without women, even it some means could be found of propagating the race without them. Most of the trade of the world would come to a standstill ... Women keep the world going in more ways than one, and if they are the supreme civilisers they are also the greatest shoppers and buyers of the world.

To a large extent it rests with us which industries we choose to encourage and which we choose to ignore. Hitherto we have been curiously unintelligent in our shopping. Too often we have bought as cheaply as we could, without asking ourselves any of the questions that as citizens we are bound to ask. We have taken little or no trouble to inform ourselves where such or such an article is made, or under what conditions it was made; and if it happens to be very cheap we are pleased with our 'wonderful bargain', quite forgetting that it is pretty sure to be produced under sweated conditions and probably in a foreign country. In defence of this attitude of mind, we must remember that even the saving of one penny a day is a matter of importance in thousands of British homes. There are other who would certainly consider it desirable to save a shilling a day, if possible. On the one hand we do want to buy British goods, at a fair price; on the other, we must try and buy as cheaply as we can.

We come to a third category of people – not in the majority at present – who are seriously concerned at the state of British trade and who are anxious, even at a sacrifice to themselves, to buy in the home market. This is not always as easy as it sounds. I tried to buy some Canadian tinned salmon recently, 'at any rate', I said, 'it must be Empire salmon'. The grocer's boy said he was very sorry but they only stocked tinned salmon from Newfoundland!

I pointed out that if he had been to Wembley he would have know that Newfoundland was part of the Empire, and fondly hope that he will be better informed on the next occasion. Again, I asked my housekeeper one morning to get me some Empire tinned fruit. I said as she left, 'Remember, I don't want American tinned goods.' She returned in triumph with California peaches; again I pointed out that California did not acknowledge the Union Jack, and next time I shall have Australian fruit on the table.

WHERE WE FAIL

If every Member of the Over-Seas League and their friends would buy Empire food, English chocolate, matches, tooth paste, tobacco, stockings and hundreds of other things, we should very soon help to bring back prosperity to our country and to our Empire. What a fine New Year's resolution that would be for us all! But there is another point not to be overlooked. If we are to wake up our manufacturers, we must continue to buy foreign goods when they are *better made and more beautiful* than our own.

The lessons of the Paris Exhibition of Decorative Arts have been almost entirely lost by us as a people. One of the organisers of the British Section predicts that because 'the tremendous wave has been swept across Europe, from Poland to Denmark, and from Sweden to the shores of the Mediterranean, has passed these islands by', the wave that is of modern feeling in decorative art in two years' time 90 per cent of the shops of the world will be filled with goods of foreign manufacture, and not with British. We shall have been left far behind in the race. It is well that we should buy British goods: but it is not well that we should lower our standard and buy the productions of our own country if they are vulgar in design and poor in feeling, when we might buy something of foreign manufacture that is beautiful, both in design and workmanship.

Perrier advertisement from *Overseas*, Aug. 1917, back page.

The
SHIRT
on which
the sun
never
sets

ALL over the world "Viyella" shirts are covering the shoulders that are bearing the burden of Empire.

The Briton abroad—to whom chills and colds, arising from changes of temperature, are often a very dangerous business — welcomes the unique protective qualities of "Viyella" fine twill flannel.

He appreciates, too, the easy fit and sturdy strength of these soft, fine-textured Shirts from Home.

For all the freedom they give for his more active life—"Viyella" Shirts are thoroughly in accord with that British tradition of trim, well-groomed appearance under all circumstances and at all times.

Even primitive native washing methods cannot spoil their rich, "fresh-from-the-shirtmaker's" appearance.

Prices ruling in Great Britain

Tunic Shirts - - **16/6**
Tennis Shirts - **18/-**
Pyjamas - - - **29/6**

Always see name "Viyella" on woven tab sewn in garment.

FROM FIRST - CLASS SHIRTMAKERS AND OUTFITTERS.

"Viyella" Tennis Socks— made from the same yarn as the famous flannel— are equally satisfying. **From 2/6 per pair.**

If any difficulty in obtaining, please write for address of suitable retailer to

Wm. Hollins & Co. Ltd. (suppliers to Trade only), 741 Viyella House, Old Change, Cheapside, London, E.C. 4.

"Viyella" Shirts
(Regd)

unshrinkable fine twill flannel

§ *BRITISH AND GUARANTEED.*

Viyella Shirts advertisement from *Overseas*, Aug. 1928, p.1.

EVEN IF YOU'RE THEOTHER SIDE OF THE WORLD

YOU CAN BE SURE OF A FINE LEAVE CAR

The world's a small place, but England is a big island—when you're home only for a few fleeting months. Then, a really reliable car from Henlys, England's greatest leave-car experts, will double the pleasure of your leave and halve the expense of getting about. Henlys offer you the finest selection of cars, New and Used, and the greatest facilities. Write them now for booklet and full particulars of the advantages offered, including combined hire-purchase and re-purchase terms. Or, when you arrive in London call at one of Henlys' showrooms.

HENLYS

England's Leading Motor Agents, Devonshire House, Piccadilly, London, England. Phone : Grosvenor 2271. And at Manchester, Bristol, Bournemouth.

Henlys advertisement from *Overseas*, Jan. 1935, p.ix.

The Month's Cartoons

FROM THE AMERICAN POINT OF VIEW.

" Is everybody in this country 100 per cent. American, mother ? "
" Why, of course not, child. Somebody has to do the work."

From New York *Life*.

THE PILOT WHO WOULDN'T BE DROPPED.
(With acknowledgments to *Punch*.)
From the London *Daily Express*.

MARS, THE EVER VORACIOUS.
From *Il 420* (Florence).

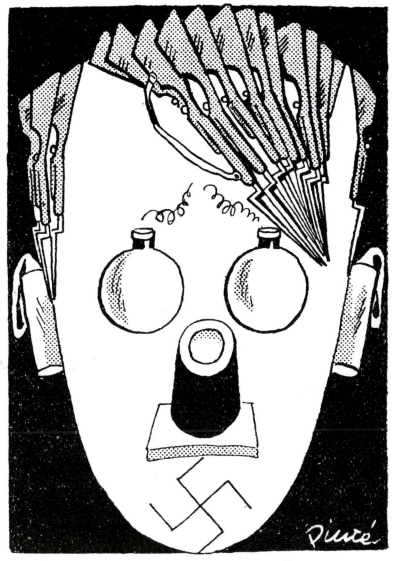

HITLER—IN THE FRENCH LOOKING-
GLASS.

From *Maygarzag* (Budapest).

A cartoon from *Overseas*, Jun. 1934, p.19.

During the 1920s and 1930s the magazine combined details of League activities at home and abroad, advertisements, contact addresses and photographs with a similar interest in wider political and social issues, creating an excellent record of the period from a 'Middle England' point of view. There were well-known and sometimes controversial contributors, but Evelyn Wrench, as editor, kept the balance with professional skill. In this he was helped by the assistant editor, Eric Chaplin, who worked for the magazine for 17 years. There was a constant record of numbers of members in every edition, in the early years illustrated by the 'Over-Seas Club Tree'. Evelyn Wrench's passion for figures even extended at one point to recording the number of meals served in the Buttery each month. However dazzling the published figures, it is nevertheless sometimes difficult to be certain of their accuracy.

Early on, Wrench had aimed at a reading public of 450,000 from a circulation of 23,000–30,000 members. He always had in mind the part that *Overseas* could play, not only in providing entertainment and practical contact, but in spreading the word of the Empire brotherhood. A quotation from John Ruskin, 'imperialism synonymous with social service', was a favourite maxim of Evelyn Wrench. Ruskin's ideas were a source of inspiration to him.

Evelyn Wrench gave up the editorship of *Overseas* of necessity during the 1939–45 war. He was succeeded first by Eric Chaplin and then by two professional editors, Tom Iremonger, MP (retired in 1982) and Elwyn Hartley Edwards. The wartime magazine continued to appear monthly in reduced form and whilst recording the immense range of activity at Over-Seas House and the fund-raising initiatives (Field Forces Hampers, the Tobacco Fund and the like) it still looked at larger issues, for example in the regular feature 'The month in the Empire' and other articles of interest such as 'Boy miners in training at New Court Colliery in Coalville'. Visits of eminent people to the headquarters, such as the Viceroy of India, Lord Wavell, were also recorded.

The OVER-SEAS *Membership* TREE

The Membership Tree has added five more ripened fruits to its branches, thanks to the enrolment of 473 further new Members, whose names appear in this number.

Thus 1,046 new Members have been enrolled since the 25th Birthday campaign was first announced, one-tenth of the total of 10,000 which we hope to reach in celebration of the 25th birthday of the League, August 27th, 1935.

There are now 14 months left in which to enrol 9,000 new Members. About 650 new Members each month will be required. Can we do it ?

Junior Members, who enrol for the sum of 5s. before the age of 18, are not, of course, included in our figures, though we are happy to announce that over 70 have joined during the past two months.

A coloured and mounted copy of the Tree, with 50 fruits on its branches each representing one Member, is being sent to all Branches and H.C.S.'s of the League ; and a number of smaller trees, with 12 fruits, have been prepared to send to individual enthusiasts on our roll of membership. We shall be glad to send one to any Member who is willing to help with the 25th Birthday Drive.

PLEASE HELP US TO DARKEN AT LEAST SIX NEW FRUITS IN THE
JULY NUMBER

Total required	10,000
Two months' enrolment	1,046
Balance required	8,954

The Over-Seas Club Tree demonstrated the growth of membership month by month, from *Overseas*, Jun. 1934, p.18.

After the war, the magazine still retained its Macdonald Gill cover. Serious articles such as 'Australia in the atomic age', 'Empire into Commonwealth' and 'The coal crisis' reflected the mood and concerns of the post-war world. With the retirement of Evelyn Wrench, the magazine became less personal, his monthly letter becoming first 'This month's events', subsequently the 'Chairman's message' and later the 'Director General's monthly message'. The magazine continued to attract distinguished contributors during this period.

By the 1950s the cost of sending the magazine to all members became a problem and members in this period were asked to request a copy. Further economies later in the decade saw the magazine appearing bi-monthly and, later, quarterly.

In 1951 Tom Iremonger introduced a variation for the cover. The trademark Macdonald Gill artwork disappeared to be replaced by tasteful photographs of Commonwealth scenes. Serious articles about the Commonwealth, and themed editorials on countries such as Scotland, Ulster, Pakistan and Australia, made the slimmer magazine more formal and professional.

Further cutbacks followed in the 1960s, with the introduction of a newspaper format, a loss of general articles and advertising and a decline in appearance. The Chairman's message was an important feature and the usual reports on Branch and League activities kept contact alive. Home members were asked to pay 5*s.* a year to receive the magazine, so difficult was the League's financial position at this time.

In the early 1980s, the magazine became the responsibility of successive PR directors with external editorial and design help. The format only changed more radically when Pat Treasure, PR Director from 1988, gradually initiated more Commonwealth coverage, largely through the contacts she had made when attending the Commonwealth conference at Harare as League representative in 1991. With a bigger budget for articles and pictures, plus a new design format, *Overseas* became much more professional.

The cover of *Overseas* in Nov. 1956.

Pat Treasure became the full-time editor from 1994, and was able to concentrate on obtaining articles from Commonwealth journalists and League members with specific interests such as the Arts, which made the journal more focused. At the same time, particular aspects of the ROSL and Commonwealth life were realised in more face-to-face interviews, including some with artists and musicians. Vicky Baker continued the modernising process, changing the format where appropriate and experimenting with improved photography and layout. Miranda Moore has developed this style, rationalising the content to make it more accessible and returning to a more serious examination of Commonwealth and other problems, typical of the pre-war magazine. The modern *Overseas* is a readable publication covering the traditional topics in a professional way with excellent photographs and relevant and appealing articles.

The Travelling Secretary

When Evelyn Wrench returned from his 17-month tour of the Commonwealth in 1913, he was convinced that this exhausting undertaking had in fact been the true beginning of the Over-Seas movement and that the 1910 foundation had been a prelude to the real business. He realised that regular personal contact between the headquarters and the branches and Honorary Corresponding Secretaries was necessary to avoid misunderstandings, encourage membership and to keep the enthusiasm for the Empire project alive. The magazine *Overseas* already in prospect would be important but there could be no substitute for personal contact.

The First World War stopped the development of this idea temporarily, but by 1922, with the Over-Seas League well established, the need for a Travelling Secretary to revisit old branches and create new ones was of first importance. Eric Rice (who was associated with the Club from 1918 to 1946) was the first appointment. His links with the League developed during the 1920s and 1930s, not only as Travelling Secretary, almost perpetually on tour, but also being in charge of the Men's Annexe in Park Place. In this capacity he organised receptions and welcomed visitors, eventually becoming Assistant Secretary to Evelyn Wrench and, on Wrench's retirement, Secretary (i.e. Director General) of the Over-Seas League. The extent of his tours is remarkable by today's standards and would not have been possible without the generous hospitality offered by overseas members.

The tours were not confined to the Commonwealth, however. In 1931 Rice's tour took in Venice, Athens, Istanbul, Singapore, Cyprus, Beirut, Damascus, Jerusalem, Haiti, Jaffa and Cairo. More typically, in 1926 a tour of the Commonwealth and other countries worldwide lasted eight months and added 1,000 new members to the League. In the 1930s, his duties at Over-Seas House being demanding, an additional travelling Secretary, Lisle Carr, was appointed, to be followed by Philip Crawshaw, later Director General of the ROSL. Eric Rice had a monthly column in *Overseas*, 'A diary of a travelling secretary', which reflected his experiences and, more importantly, the number of new members these voyages had produced. Eric Rice noted that in his first ten years in the job – in his own words 'A task demanding Funds of humour, pertinacity and tact' and 'A cast iron constitution' – he had travelled 260,000 miles. He was awarded an OBE for his work in 1935.

Evelyn Wrench also travelled frequently throughout the Commonwealth, and Council members volunteered for special assignments when visiting branches abroad. The connections between the home and overseas branches of the League were thus regularly maintained.

After the Second World War changes in the costs associated with travelling and the development of better and newer forms of communication made the role of Travelling Secretary much less important. Once Philip Crawshaw became Director General he undertook Commonwealth tours himself, accompanied by his wife, and a Travelling Secretary was no longer needed. A video of their six-and-a-half-month tour in 1961 provides an excellent record of

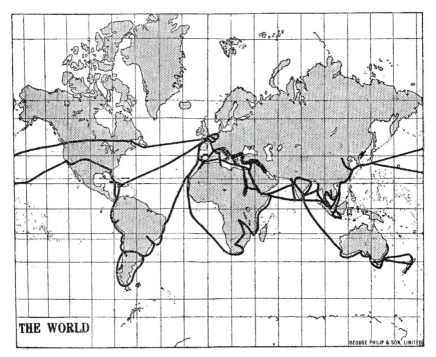

Eric Rice's map of his journeys on the League's behalf in 1934.

the range of such visits and the amount of hospitality received. This practice was to be followed subsequently by later Director Generals, Chairmen and sometimes Council members with particular interest in Commonwealth countries. Increasingly, tours were extended worldwide once more, with the present Director General having travelled more widely than his more recent predecessors, making many more contacts. In the early years, however, the Travelling Secretary was the vital link between the League's headquarters and its overseas members.

In 1939, the mother of Eric Rice became ill unexpectedly, and he was unable to go ahead with his planned tour of India, Malaysia, Singapore and China. A young substitute was hastily engaged and, with minimal instructions, sent out on the P&O liner *Strathallan* to take Rice's place. This was Philip Noakes, a 23-year-old Cambridge graduate. Thanks to his diaries and records we have a remarkable insight into the whole project.[3] A star at Cambridge, President of the Union, Noakes' only overseas experience at the time was a university debating tour of the USA, sponsored by the ROSL, during which he encountered much anti-war and anti-European feeling. In this sense, Philip Noakes was better prepared for this tough assignment than the average young man of his age. Nonetheless his letters show a lack of briefing that would have daunted a lesser man. (He had written earlier in desperation to Eric Rice, 'I feel about as knowledgeable as if I was being asked to convert Mars!')

Sped on his way by a telegram of support from Sir Evelyn and Lady Wrench, he spent his first days aboard organising a cocktail party under the Captain's auspices to introduce the Over-Seas League to passengers. He records the 'need to be ruthless' and wasted no time in recruiting 50 new members. He was also constantly meeting existing members during the voyage, including a relative of Evelyn Wrench. He wrote to his fiancée, at home, 'Yes she is a relation of *the* Wrenches and has the same sort of face! She is a rather remote cousin and her family live in Delhi and were all roped in by Eric Rice three years ago!' Less happily, he comments on a fellow passenger, 'a rather horrid old man turns out to be a Life Member – tho' he courteously explained that he thought the Royal Empire Society much better!' Vivid impressions of people bring the voyage to life – including several Lords on board and a Maharajah who turned out to be a Life Member (Noakes signed up the rest of his entourage during the trip) and the hard-drinking English military returning to post 'who talk as if they owned India' – and all combine to convey his gradual growth in confidence and ability to cope with the situation.

Once the ship docked in Bombay, a Gurkha who was Eric Rice's usual bearer on his Indian visits arrived to welcome Philip Noakes and accompany him on his tour, making all domestic arrangements. He formed the charming habit of putting up the photograph of Noake's fiancée, Moragh Dickson, at every stop, to make him feel at home. A pattern for the tour emerged; success entirely depended on the individual Honorary Corresponding Secretaries in the various regions. A good organiser would have first-class introductions at the highest level, enabling Philip Noakes to organise meetings and receptions at prestigious locations including Government House. The prestige of the Over-Seas League on the sub-continent is clearly demonstrated. The Delhi meetings were some of the most successful despite the strong National Party movement for Indian independence, which made the attraction of membership of an Empire organisation more dubious. This success was largely due to the indefatigable HCS in Delhi, Colonel Webb-Johnson, described by Noakes as

> … fearfully energetic. He knows everyone in Delhi and if I haven't met them all, it won't be his fault … My party was amazing – Cabinet Ministers, Congressmen, a Judge or two, Mrs Sorarji Nehru, poet and politician, Colonels, majors, shop keepers, saris, beards and English ladies.

Later he said that in contrast to some of his experiences, 'I have had here the sense that I am doing something real and worthwhile.' The Viceroy agreed to become a vice-president of the League and Noakes made contact with many members of the National Assembly, including Pandit Nehru's sisters:

> The dinner with Nehru's sisters and party was most pleasant but as someone said quite truly to me, the intelligent Indian has given up trying to make the English take him seriously and so does not take him seriously either.

On the other hand, Noakes had success with the British Establishment, enrolling His Excellency the Commander-in-Chief, India ('a dear old man'), as a Life Member. Throughout he reveals a mature perception of the political situation, privately noting that 'The British Government have made an awful mess of India.' Following his instincts, Philip Noakes altered the tone of his addresses, stressing the non-political character of the League and presenting it as 'the largest and most democratic of all societies of the British

Commonwealth'. His emphasis on 'good feeling and mutual respect' between the Commonwealth and Great Britain was very much in keeping with Evelyn Wrench's own views and greatly increased support for and the popularity of the League in India, his press coverage in Indian newspapers being particularly impressive.

Noakes made the most of his old college contacts, Queensmen both Indian and English crop up regularly in his accounts, he wrote newspaper articles about the political situation in Europe and the Far East, broadcast for 12 minutes on All India Radio, and recorded that he left India with 250 new members (membership being everything to Evelyn Wrench, Philip Noakes had been set a target of gaining 100 new members a month). Noakes was summoned to Bombay to meet the Wrenches, who were en route to Australia. Sir Evelyn became seriously ill and eventually was obliged to return home. Philip Noakes records his impression of Evelyn Wrench as: 'distinguished and courteous showing, despite his illness, a constant interest in ideas and plans'.

During this epic four months, Philip Noakes on his own initiative went on to Singapore, Malaya and the Far East, completing his League commission and only returning in July 1939 prior to the outbreak of war. He married his fiancée, Moragh Dickson, in January 1940 and went on to have a distinguished career both in the War and later in the Colonial Office, subsequently the Foreign and Commonwealth Office. After the war he maintained his connection with the ROSL as an influential and highly respected member of the Central Council.

Noakes' letters provide an insight into the difficulties the Travelling Secretary could experience, which called for independence, judgement and innovation on his part. The support and generosity of overseas members, and particularly the HCSs, was also significant, as was the esteem in which the League was held generally. The Travelling Secretary provided the vital link between the headquarters and the Commonwealth, demonstrating 'good feeling and mutual respect'.

Below and opposite: Headlines in Indian, Malayan and Singapore newspapers give widespread publicity to the League and Philip Noakes' visit.

THE MALAYA TRIBUNE, WEDNESDAY, MAY 24, 1939.

Overseas League Travelling Secretary In Singapore

Singapore, Wednesday.

BECAUSE of the importance of Singapore, making it an ideal centre for the work of the Overseas League, Mr. P. R. Noakes, the Travelling Secretary of the League, who arrived to-day by the "Karapara," is going to spend a month here.

Mr. Noakes who is twenty-three years old left Cambridge last year, where he took an Arts course. He was the President of the Cambridge Union and in that capacity toured the various American Universities.

The Overseas League, founded in 1910, in a Society of British people whose object is the promotion of goodwill and understanding among the various people of the Empire. It has a membership of 5,000.

Singapore has 350 members, while there is an equivalent number in the rest of Malaya. Mr. Noakes' aim in coming here is to meet members of the League, to make it better known to Singaporeans and to secure more members.

While in India, where he spent three months, Mr. Noakes personally enrolled no fewer than 300 new members for the League and despite the seemingly adverse political conditions there he received a great deal of help from the Indian National Congress.

As a demonstration of goodwill the Leader of the Opposition in the Legislative Assembly, Mr. Desai, became a member. Mr. Noakes also visited Burma, where he spent a few days before arriving here.

Mr. Noakes will also visit various centres in the Malay States after which he will return to London.

Mr. J. Wilmott, the Singapore secretary of the Overseas League, welcomed Mr. Noakes on his arrival here.

The Overseas League is having a dinner at the Sea View Hotel to-night. Mr. Noakes will speak

Friendly League Without Politics — 50,000 Members

From Our Special Correspondent

NEW DELHI, March 16.

Mr. Phillip Noakes, Travelling Secretary of the Overseas League, who has been staying at 6, Akbar Road, with Mr. S. Webb Johnson, Honorary Corresponding Secretary in Delhi and Simla, has received the support of H. E. The Viceroy and Lady Linlithgow, who have accepted the position of Vice-Presidents of the League. Others who supported the League during Mr. Noakes' visit to Delhi or who have recently joined the League are H. E. The Commander-in-Chief, the Hon'ble Chief Justice of India, the Air Officer Commanding in India, Sir Mohammad Zafrullah Khan, the Hon'ble Sir Maneckji Dadabhoy, Mr. Bhulabhai Desai.

One of the main objects of the League, which is a non-political organization of over 50,000 members, is to promote good feeling and respect between the peoples and communities, and it recognises no distinction of class or creed. The service given at home and overseas to its members, and the Oversea Journal, are already

LOCAL ENGAGEMENTS

NOTICES IN THIS COLUMN ARE INSERTED AT TWO RUPEES PER LINE

LINK IN WORLD ORGANISATION

Overseas League's Work

Members of t' Overseas League in Bombay and th .... Mr. Philip Noakes, of the League Green's Rest Tuesday even meeting, Mr. League had play in the consolidate i in Bombay.

Mr. W. correspondi League in Noakes to had been original p tour Indi necessitat suddenly Noakes's fore. to

The L don, Mr really r bers al club. organi that v city get u siasm or enth.... for

M. .... ing, stated .... why enthusiasm in the .... ing in Bombay should fizzle out. .... League had succeeded in uniting pe ple in parts of the Empire from days when it had no special organi tion, headquarters or representati The League, besides having m branches, had representatives voluntarily represented it in var centres. It had also a mag and a journal which, he bell formed a useful link between part of the world and anothe also acquainted members with League's plans.

Mr. Noakes felt that the could do useful work in B..

There were many members in the city, and as Bombay was the Gateway of the East, he felt that the League had a very definite part to play in the city. He hoped to orga- nise a way through which that could be done.

The League, Mr. Noakes de- clared, should have a more important place in India today. The political

Alexandra Road, Gamdevi, when the delegates from Bombay will speak on their general impressions of the 13th Session of the All-India Women's Conference held at Delhi, Mrs. Heera- bai Gilder will preside.

OVERSEAS LEAGUE.—A meeting will be held at Green's Hotel on Tuesday at 6-30 p.m. when members of the Lea- gue are asked to be present with their friends to meet Mr. Philip Noakes, Travelling Secretary in India, who is at present staying in Bombay with the object of obtaining support for the League. All members are asked to .... in making this occasion a suc-

"WHAT HONOUR CAN THERE BE FOR... BANDITS?"

Average Britons Think War On China Disgusting

INTERVIEW WITH OVERSEAS LEAGUE SECRETARY

Kuala Lumpur, Wednesday.

"THE average Englishman, of whom I hope I am one, thinks Japan's continued war on China to be unjustified and, he hopes, unsuccessful. He is not worried about British prestige or even British trade. He just thinks it is disgust- ing and uncivilised to attack, bomb and slaughter the de- fenceless population of another country, whatever the mo- tive. As for prestige I myself do not feel that as between ourselves and the Japanese, that we have lost face, honour or prestige, for what face, honour or prestige can there be for international bandits?"

Thus remarked Mr. Philip Noakes, Travelling Secretary of the overseas League, in an in- terview with a representative of the Malaya Tribune.

Continuing, he said:

"When I left England in January the current feeling with regard to the world situation was definitely harden- ing into a determination on the part of the normally peace-loving British men and women that the reign of lawless- ness in Europe and the Far East should be stopped.

"There was no hostility to the people of any country, but a sincere hatred of .... and .... ing to London House.

welcome at Overseas House... people in England today were be- ginning to realise the need for national service, so those interested in the League's work realised the need for Empire service, for service to the men and women who made up that Empire. The support now given to the League had enabled it to ren- der service not only to its own mem- bers but to others outside. It had sponsored many forms of social ser- vice, and was at present carrying out a scheme to train boys on farms in England for emigration as farmers overseas.

The more support it had the more privileges it could offer to its mem- bers. He appealed to members to help the League. Every member,

Overseas League

Asked about the objects and activities of the Overseas League and the object of his present visit to Malaya, he said: "The Overseas League tries to remove misunderstandings and to promote good feeling between all classes and com- munities within the British Empire".

Mr. Noakes added that the member- ship was open without distinction to all British subjects without regard to class or creed, and that all headquarters and branches and local centres of the League are available for the use of members in many parts of the world as clubs and meeting places for intelligent discussion.

The monthly "Overseas League" is read all over the world and tries to spread the League principles of under- standing and mutual service and respect.

Continuing he said, "Asiatics help the League in promoting its aims in many ways, both directly and indirectly. Many Indian, Malay and Chinese mem- bers are very enthusiastic for the League and have helped as honarary correspond- ing secretaries and on committees to run local centres for the League, thus contri- buting actively for its progress. Each member can help by supporting his local branch and by telling his friends about the League."

"We have only a few branches as yet in Malaya but I hope that there will be more support forthcoming. Singapore, Malacca, Kuala Lumpur, Ipoh and Penang have local secre- taries and there are over 1,000 mem- bers in the whole of Malaya." Mr. Noakes added that he had enrolled nearly 200 members in less than two months.

Mr. P. Noakes.

LUNCHEON PARTY.

Saturday, 25th February 1939.

Mr. Kitchin	Captain Burns
Mrs. Betham	Captain Gooch
Mr. Bridgman	The Lady Joan Hope
Mrs. Holmberg	Mr. Noakes
THE VICEROY	The Lady Anne Hope
The Lady Lilian Wemyss	The Rt.Revd.The Bishop of Lahore
The Hon.G.Hamilton-Russell	Miss Betham
The Lady Doreen Hope	Captain Chandos-Pole

Lieut.Southby, R.N.

The Marquess & Marchioness of Linlithgow

request the pleasure of

Mr. P. Noakes'

Company at Luncheon

on Saturday the 25th February

at 1-10 o'Clock.

An answer is requested to the
A.D.C. in charge of Invitations.

Philip Noakes' invitation from the Viceroy with seating plan.

Philip Noakes rides in a rickshaw during his Far Eastern tour.

Portraits of Chairmen, Past and Present

When Robert Newell became Director General in 1991 he was able to put into practice his idea of commemorating all living (and future) Chairmen of the Royal Over-Seas League appropriately by commissioning their portraits to be painted by winners or scholars of the Art Competition. This has given the ROSL the advantage of some interesting portraits of distinguished people and at the same time has encouraged the young artists, none of whom had previously been known for their portraiture. Some have since made successful careers in the genre.

The first commission was the portrait of Lord Grey of Naunton, Chairman 1976–81, President 1981–93 and Grand President 1993–99, painted by Tai-Shan Schierenberg in 1990, who was the First Prize winner in the ROSL Art Competition. This portrait is now in the entrance hall of Over-Seas House. The same year the portraits of Mr Maneck Dalal and Sir Lawrence Byford were added, and that of Sir David Scott, who donated a portrait of himself, painted by a friend. Thus all three living Chairmen were celebrated simultaneously. The following portraits now hang in the corridor and on the front staircase at the League:

- Sir David Scott, 1981–6, by Rupert Shepherd
- Mr Maneck Dalal, 1986–9, by Christian Furr
- Sir Lawrence Byford, 1989–92, by Jane Walker
- Mr Peter McEntee, 1992–5, by Melissa Scott-Miller
- Sir Geoffrey Ellerton, 1995–2000, by Robert White
- Sir Colin Imray, 2000–5, by Andrew Tift
- Mr Stanley Martin, 2005, by Nick Archer

In addition a portrait of The Queen to mark her 40th anniversary of accession hangs in the hall. Her Majesty was given a choice of the artists already represented and chose Christian Furr. This portrait was painted in 1995 and was unveiled by Lord Grey the Grand President. The recent portraits of Lady Barbirolli, OBE, the long-time Chairman of Adjudication of the Music Competition (1981–2002), is entitled *Evelyn in Her Garden* by Michael John Shaw, painted in 1995. The portrait of Lord Luce, President of the ROSL, painted by Bella Easton, completes this distinguished collection.

A recent portrait of Sir Colin Imray, Chairman 2000–5.

V

The Branches, Honorary Corresponding Secretaries and Reciprocal Clubs

ranches of the Over-Seas Club were already flourishing in Canada, Australia, New Zealand and South Africa
when John Evelyn Wrench undertook his first Empire tour
in 1912. This was partly as a result of the great interest created
throughout the Empire by the articles written by Wrench in *The
Overseas Daily Mail* prior to the founding of the Club in 1910. These
articles, encouraged by Lord Northcliffe, had described the whole
idea of such a society, open to all, as a 'Brotherhood of Service'
linking Empire citizens overseas and at home. More than 12,000
people responded, eager to join such a society when it should be
founded. The ground had thus been prepared and the initiative to
form branches followed quickly once the Club was established in
1910.

The branches were not confined to the Commonwealth
itself but were to be created wherever 'a group of members were
formally organised under a local committee'. They spread rapidly worldwide. The earliest *Overseas* magazines in 1916 record new
branches in Transvaal, Basutoland, California, Argentina, Queensland, New Zealand and the Cook Islands, Newfoundland, Nova

Scotia and Ontario, Samoa, Hong Kong, Lisbon, China and Parys South Africa. There were altogether 1,000 branches of the Over-Seas Club and Honorary Corresponding Secretaries (HCSs) throughout the world in 1917. At that time branches and HCSs were recorded together and it is difficult to separate their functions.

The rules governing the formation of a branch were simple. In 1926 these were recorded as:

> All Branches of the Over-Seas League are expected to conform to the regulations laid down by the Central Council and the terms of the Royal Charter and every member of a local branch is expected to pay the subscription of 10 shillings per annum which includes the receipt of the Society's monthly magazine *Overseas*.[1]

This format has remained essentially the same, allowing for the changes in costs through the decades that followed. Branches had premises or regular meeting places as availability and funds dictated.

Membership could be local or full (comprehensive), allowing those members the use of the facilities at Over-Seas House in London and Edinburgh and at reciprocal clubs around the world. Eventually this became the more usual form, as people travelled extensively in an era of cheap travel opportunities. Individual branches remain strongholds of ROSL life to this day.

Because there has always been a constant connection between the headquarters in London and all the branches, it was inevitable that they should develop initially as microcosms of Over-Seas House, London, in character and ideals. The priority given to support for education and the arts as well as hospitality and charitable interests has always been an essential part of branch life. There are many examples of how close the contact has been, and this is well illustrated by the letters written by Eric Rice (acting Secretary) during the Second World War to the Christchurch, NZ, branch acknowledging minute details of individual membership at the branch, with passing reference to the Blitz raging overhead at the time. Real friendships have developed between HQ staff and branch secretaries and members, enhancing the friendly informality of the League.

With time the individual character of the branches developed strongly but there have always been common features to their activities. The observance of Empire Day, later Commonwealth Day, with services in cathedrals and local churches, and receptions to mark the Sovereign's official birthday, provide important examples. There has also been a tradition of joining other Commonwealth groups – the so-called Loyal Societies – for joint activities and reciprocal events. Social events, lectures, lunches and special visits are still at the heart of branch life.

The extent to which HQ relied on the branches for organised fund-raising is illustrated by a letter from Evelyn Wrench to overseas members in April 1940, as the war in Europe began:

> I hate having to write this letter to you, but I know I can rely on your help to put the Over-Seas League in an entirely sound position, so that it may emerge stronger than ever from this period of crisis in the Nation's history.
>
> At the weekends Overseas House in London has become a real centre of welcome for the men from overseas. I think you would be very proud of your membership if you could pop in to see what we are doing.
>
> One of our members has just sent me a cheque for this year at the new rate, although not liable for it … If everyone who gets this letter would do the same, I should have no financial worries this year. I assure you running a great organisation like ours in times like this is no bed of roses…

The branches have responded with great generosity whenever called upon to do so. Not just for the many fund-raising enterprises already mentioned in this history – money for the purchase of buildings, funds for the forces and the homeless in both Wars,

Below and overleaf:
Letters of appreciation received by New Zealand branches
after the Second World War.

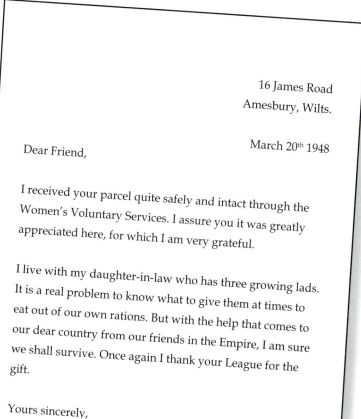

16 James Road
Amesbury, Wilts.

March 20th 1948

Dear Friend,

I received your parcel quite safely and intact through the Women's Voluntary Services. I assure you it was greatly appreciated here, for which I am very grateful.

I live with my daughter-in-law who has three growing lads. It is a real problem to know what to give them at times to eat out of our own rations. But with the help that comes to our dear country from our friends in the Empire, I am sure we shall survive. Once again I thank your League for the gift.

Yours sincerely,

W.C. Hoslett

92 Ring House
Sage Street
Shadwell, London

[undated]

Dear Miss Russell,

Just a line thanking you for the clothes. I think it was very kind of you all to think of us and I wish you all the very best of everything. I know what it is like to go short since this war. My husband had an accident and died three days later, and a few months later I was bombed out and lost everything, and lay on cold stones. Then I had my sons taken away from me in the war, I did not get much allowance to keep me and buy shoes, so I walked about with wet feet and now suffer with rheumatism. Could not go to work as I have heart trouble and since my son came home from the Far East he gets colds very quickly and cannot keep warm, but I thank God we came through the war. I don't know how to thank you all for the clothes.

Yours very very gratefully,

R. Bailey

1. *The View from Green Park*, painted by J. Whitlock in 1848. Rutland House and Vernon House are on the extreme right.

2. The ROSL Annual Scholars Exhibition on tour at Edinburgh College of Art in 1994. *Left to right*: Stephanie Sampson (Canada); Ming Wong (Singapore); Moh'd Azhar Abd Manan (Malaysia); Patrick Mazola (Kenya); and Murshida Arzu Alpana (Bangladesh).

3. Portrait of the former League President Lord Grey of Naunton,
Chairman 1976–81, later President 1981–93 and Grand President 1993–9,
painted by Tai-Shan Schierenberg in 1990.

4. Sir Alan Bowness, Director of the Tate Gallery, with Philip Davies, First Prize winner at ROSL Annual Exhibition 1986 with the prizewinning work *Shelter*.

5. Lauren Porter, with *Hunting Trophies*, inspired by her ROSL scholarship study trip to Canada, pictured at the ROSL Annual Exhibition 2008, held at gallery@oxo on London's South Bank.

6. Lady Barbirolli with her portrait and the artist Michael John Shaw.

7. Portrait of
Mr Maneck Dalal,
Chairman 1986–9,
by Christian Furr.

8. Yvonne
Adhiambo Owuor,
winner of the 2003
Caine Prize for
African Writing
(supported by
ROSL ARTS)
for 'Weight of
Whispers',
beside a bust of Sir
Michael Caine.

9. Lord Luce, President of ROSL, with flautist Laura Lucas, Gold Medal and First Prize winner, ROSL Annual Music Competition 2007, and Gavin Henderson, Chairman of Adjudicators.

10. New Zealand Director Lyn Milne at a Gala Concert at Government House, Wellington, in 2007 celebrating the Pettman/ROSL ARTS Scholarship for a NZ Chamber Ensemble. The Governor General the Hon. Sir Anand Satyanand is on her left.

11. BackBeat percussion ensemble (Simone Rebello and Damien Harron) perform at a ROSL concert at the Millennium Dome in 2000.

12. A view of the stage in the refurbished Princess Alexandra Hall with ROSL prizewinners cellist Gemma Resefield and pianist Simon Lepper.

13. Over-Seas House, London: a view from the park in springtime.

14. Over-Seas House, London: the familiar front entrance in Park Place.

15. Over-Seas House, London: the Central Lounge with the Gibbs staircase.

16. View of Edinburgh Castle from the windows of 100, Princes Street.

17. Director-General, Robert Newell, with HM The Queen at the Lancaster House Concert in 1992 to mark the 40th anniversary of The Queen's accession and of the ROSL Annual Music Competition.

18. Her Majesty with performers from the Solomon Islands and Tonga at the Lancaster House concert in 1992.

19. A learner on the way to the ROSL supported Katora Primary School at the foot of the Spitzkoppe in the Namib Desert, Namibia.

20. ROSL Namibia project coordinators Margaret Adrian-Vallance and Dick Chamberlain with donated books at the start of the project.

21. ROSL bursary recipient Cwisa Cwi, far right, with pupils and teachers at Denlui School in the Nyae Nyae pointing out a tree brought down by elephants in the night.

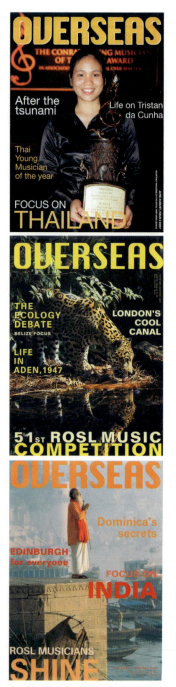

22. 'Overseas Covers the World' – some recent, colourful examples of the jackets of Overseas magazine.

and the purchase of aeroplanes, but also sponsorship of individuals, particularly young people in the fields of education, charity and the arts. The constant hospitality always on offer has also enabled the work of the League to continue successfully. The frontier spirit of welcoming the visitor has had a long life. The Second World War reinforced the ties considerably, with servicemen and women returning to Commonwealth countries having enjoyed the welcome provided by home branches as well as HQ. It could be said that, as a result, the 1950s and 1960s were the heyday of branch life.

With time and the granting of independence to many Commonwealth countries, the number of branches diminished, but their essential character has remained. Indeed, the new branches in Switzerland, Hong Kong and Thailand, and the new or revived branches in Toronto and Vancouver, the Ontario chapter and British Columbia chapter, testify to the strength of the idea. There is still a tradition of individual branches supporting their own particular charities as well as contributing to ROSL sponsorship.

In 1935, 25 years after the foundation of the ROSL, there were many branches including 30 with premises or club facilities and several hundred Corresponding Secretaries. In 1960, 50 years after the foundation, there were 61 branches, 21 with premises (see map overleaf). Today there are 28 branches marking the centenary. Activities have remained remarkably constant, as references to *Overseas* magazine and annual reports over the century testify. ROSL branches today continue in that tradition.

News in Brief from the UK Branches

Bath: Formed in the 1930s, the Bath branch has been very active in its support of ROSL aims. As recently as 2008 the Bath branch staged a concert for members in the elegant Georgian surroundings of the Bath Royal Literary and Scientific Institution, featuring the ROSL Music Competition prizewinners, the Cappa Quartet. Guests included the deputy Lord Lieutenant and County Councillors.

THE ROYAL OVER-SEAS LEAGUE

WORLD HEADQUARTERS: Over-Seas House, St. James's, London, s

CANADA
NEW BRUNSWICK
Moncton
NEWFOUNDLAND
St. John's
ALBERTA
Edmonton
Ponoka
ONTARIO
Peterborough
BRITISH COLUMBIA
Vancouver
Victoria
Ottawa
PROVINCE OF QUEBEC
Montreal

UNITED KINGDOM
(See inset)

BELGIU
Brussels
FINLAN
Karis
FRANCE
Cannes
Paris
HOLLA
Amsterdam
ITALY
Verbania-P

U.S.A.
INDIANA
Lafayette
Logansport
NEW YORK
New York
WASHINGTON
Seattle

TORONTO

WEST INDIES
BERMUDA
Hamilton

VALE

MEXICO
Mexico City
Puebla

BARBADOS
Bridgetown
HAITI
Port au Prince
JAMAICA
Kingston
LEEWARD IS
Antigua

NETHERLANDS ANTILLES
Curacao
TRINIDAD
San Fernando
WINDWARD IS
Dominica

AFRICA
GHANA
Accra
NIGERIA
Lagos
Port Harcourt

EL SALVADOR
San Salvador

SOUTH AMERICA
ARGENTINE
Bahia Blanca
Buenos Aires
Santa Elena
BRAZIL
Santos
Sao Paulo
Rio de Janeiro
COLOMBIA
Bogota
URUGUAY
Paysandu
VENEZUELA
Caracas

NORTHERN R
Broken Hill
Lusaka
NYASALAND
Limbe
Zomba
SOUTHERN R
Bulawayo

SOUTH
CAPE TOW

CAPE PROVINCE
Middleburg
Paael
Port Elizabeth
Queenstown
NATAL
Durban
Highbury
Ladysmith
Pietermaritzburg

ORA
Bethle
Frankf
Westm
TRA
Johar
Pretor
Venter
ZUL
Eshowe

KEY: Branches which have premises are shown thus . . . . LONDON
Branches without premises are shown thus . . . . **Vancouver**
Honorary Corresponding Secretaries are shown thus . . . *Zanzibar*

Note: The term BRANCH signifies a group of members of the League formally organised under a local Comm

ROSL's branches worldwide at the 50th anniversary in 1960.

UNITED KINGDOM

ULSTER
Ballycastle, Co. Antrim
Larne, Co. Antrim
Londonderry
Newcastle, Co. Down

ISLE OF MAN
Douglas

WALES
Swansea

EDINBURGH

GLASGOW

BELFAST

NOTTINGHAM

CARDIFF

LONDON

TORQUAY

SCOTLAND
Aberdeen	Kirkcaldy
Brechin, Angus	Lanark
Crieff	Lerwick, Shetland Islands
Castle Douglas	Moffat
Dundee	Perth
Inverness	Stornoway
Kilmarnock	Stranraer

ENGLAND
	Minehead
Bath	Oxford
Bournemouth	Pangbourne
Birmingham	Penzance
Bristol	Plymouth
Cheltenham	St. Austell
Derby	Sheffield
Eastbourne	Southport
Exeter	Stratford-on-Avon
Grimsby	Taunton
Liskeard	Teignmouth
Liverpool	Weston-super-Mare
Manchester	Worthing

E
A
VAY

UGAL
nd Oporto

e Mallorca
EN
m
ZERLAND
x

YPRUS
magusta

IRAQ
Basrah

PERSIAN
GULF
Bahrain
Kuwait

ADEN
Aden

NYA
basa
robi

DAN
toum

NGANYIKA
es-Salaam
rwa

ANDA
pala

NZIBAR
zibar

BURY

Lourenco
Marques

A

ATE

PAKISTAN
Chittagong
Hyderabad
Karachi
Lahore
Motijheel, Dacca
Mirpur Khas

INDIA
Assam Valley, Assam
Bombay
Calcutta
Darjeeling
Delhi
Doom Dooma, Assam
Indore
Kolar Gold Fields
Madras
Ootacamund
Patna
Tuticorin

CEYLON
Colombo
Kegalle

MAURITIUS
Port Louis

FAR EAST
BRUNEI
Seria
BURMA
Bassein
Moulmein
Rangoon
HONG KONG
Hong Kong
MALAYA
Penang
PHILIPPINES
Manila
SINGAPORE
Singapore

AUSTRALIA

BRISBANE

SYDNEY

PERTH

ADELAIDE

MELBOURNE

HOBART

NEW SOUTH WALES
Grafton
Newcastle
QUEENSLAND
Mackay
Toowoomba
Townsville

SOUTH AUSTRALIA
Far North
TASMANIA
Burnie
VICTORIA
Bendigo

NEW ZEALAND

NORTH ISLAND
Gisborne
Hamilton
Hastings
Palmerston North
Whangarei

SOUTH ISLAND
Invercargill
Oamaru
Timaru

FIJI
Suva

AUCKLAND

WELLINGTON

CHRISTCHURCH

DUNEDIN

Bournemouth: The Bournemouth branch has been holding an annual garden party in the garden of one of its members for the past 14 years, with special guests. These are always memorable and happy occasions. Bournemouth branch is remarkable for the genuine friendships formed. It has entertained many distinguished visitors, including most Chairmen of the ROSL and the late President, Lord Grey.

Cheltenham: The Cheltenham branch has been in existence since 1947. It holds afternoon meetings once a month with illustrated talks followed by tea. There is a special lunch on Commonwealth Day, a summer party, and a Christmas lunch plus occasional garden parties, as for The Queen's Golden Jubilee. It has lots of outings and long weekends at Over-Seas London or Edinburgh, which are special events.

West Cornwall: Founded in 1949, the branch has supported a locally based charity called Shelterbox, which was formed in 2001. It has become a major charity for humanitarian aid following the Indonesian tsunami disaster in 2005. It provides rapid and essential aid and has earned an outstanding international reputation. Shelterbox representatives give graphic accounts at branch meetings on this vital relief work.

Edinburgh: The Edinburgh branch, formed between the wars, continues to make progress with capacity audiences for regular functions such as the Burns Supper, Scottish Members' Dinner and St Andrew's Day Dinner. The Bridge Club and Mah Jong group meet regularly and coffee mornings have attracted a number of interesting speakers, with substantial donations being made to the RNLI and other charities.

Recent highlights have been the Commonwealth Day lunch and the popular Arts Lunch programme with distinguished speakers including the new Director of the Edinburgh Festival, Mr Jonathan Mills, and Ms Margo Macdonald, MSP. ROSL ARTS provide high-quality programmes including the Edinburgh Festival series of concerts, as well as gala evenings and Music with a View concerts.

There are many enjoyable activities combined with the Glasgow branch.

Glasgow and West of Scotland Branch: Formed in the 1930s, the Glasgow and West of Scotland branch recently highlighted the League's links with the Commonwealth in two different ways. The first occasion was a joint Arts Lunch at the Edinburgh Club House, which was also attended by representatives of the Scots–Australian Council. The speaker Ian Robert, Glasgow branch treasurer, described the creation of 'The Singing Line', Australia's first transcontinental link by undersea cable, which brought the young country into contact with the Britain and the western world.

The second event was the support given to the Malawi project – an outstanding initiative by pupils of Holyrood Secondary School (and its feeder primaries) in Glasgow, raising £70,000 to send senior pupils to a village in Malawi to buy materials and help construct a three-classroom block. This was done in conjunction with Mary's Meals to provide one vitamin-supplemented meal per day to all the pupils.

Exeter: The Exeter branch, one of the very first ever ROSL branches (founded in 1916), holds monthly lunches from September to April followed by a talk. There is a coffee morning in June and a picnic in July, plus concerts organised with ROSL ARTS for celebrations such as for The Queen's Jubilee and her 80th birthday. A special initiative has been the erection of a plaque in Gaudy Street, Exeter, to commemorate the two colonial pioneers David Collins and George P. Harris, immortalised in New South Wales and Tasmania, who were born and brought up in the street. This plaque was originally suggested by a League member in Victoria, Australia, and the Exeter branch put the idea into practice.

West Sussex: Since 1994 the West Sussex branch and the Eastbourne branch have agreed to sponsor jointly a prize in the League's Music Competition, known as the Sussex Prize. After the Eastbourne branch was disbanded, West Sussex continued its support with a constant contribution to the prize. In May each year, branch members attend the Brighton Festival to support ROSL Competition prizewinners giving a lunchtime concert there.

Taunton: Taunton branch was founded in 1937 so has passed its Diamond Jubilee. The founding may have been connected to the return of the Somerset Light Infantry from India at independence. Since the Regiment had served in India on and off since 1824 there would be many associated civilians who then followed it home and wanted to maintain Commonwealth ties. In 2007 the Branch held a celebratory lunch in the presence of the Lord Lieutenant of Somerset and the Director General of the League. Over 70 members attended. Taunton branch looks forward to its next 60 years!

Worldwide News

Australia

Historically ROSL membership in Australia has been very strong. Its worthy aims of supporting the ideals of the Commonwealth appeal to Australians to this day and membership remains strong. There are now six branches: Queensland, New South Wales, Tasmania, Victoria, South Australia and Western Australia. Branch members enjoy local social events and all the other benefits of membership associated with belonging to the League. Through the Victoria branch financial support is provided to the Australian Singing Competition for a scholarship for a young Australian singer to visit the League in London for a master class and to perform concerts. Branches across Australia seek to support artistic endeavours and encourage young people to develop their abilities. Performing arts scholarships, art competitions, musical performances and concerts are all part of the Australian branches' activities and purposes for fund-raising. The most active branches ensure that their members are kept well informed of altruistic endeavours and seek their support and assistance. Most branches are also involved actively with their Council of British and Commonwealth Societies or their equivalent, which means they have interaction with a variety of organisations. They are honoured that the State Governors provide patronage to their local branches and that the Governor-General is Patron of the League in Australia. The League branch in Australia remains loyal to Commonwealth ideals and to the Head of the Commonwealth, HM The Queen, and aims to further the values of the ROSL in Australia into the League's second century.

Canadian Chapters

Alberta: One of the outstanding highlights of recent years for the Alberta chapter was the visit of HM The Queen to Alberta for the centenary celebrations in May 2005. The Alberta chapter has been fortunate to be included in many functions for visiting royalty and other dignitaries. Four Chairmen of the League have visited Edmonton in recent years, and they have enjoyed regular visits from the Director General. The chapter is currently looking at new initiatives in keeping with the aims and ideals of the League.

British Columbia: Founded in the mid-1990s with the BC Lieutenant-Governor the Hon Garde Gardom as patron, the British Columbia chapter has become very active since 2006. A highlight was the Christmas lunch in 2007, attended by the Vancouver pianist Grace Mo, a prizewinner in the ROSL Music Competition who gave a recital for members a few days later.

Ontario: Also founded in the mid-1990s, the Ontario chapter holds regular events and an annual lunch in Toronto to which many distinguished speakers are invited, including Former Prime Minister John Turner, the British High Commissioner to Canada; the Ontario Chief Justice; the Ontario Lieutenant Governor; the Chairman of the ROSL; and the Director General of the ROSL. In the evening following the lunches members attended a musical soirée featuring Canadian prizewinners from the ROSL Music Competition.

Hong Kong

There have always been ROSL members in Hong Kong but the branch only came into being just over a decade ago (originally founded in 1916, it closed in the early 1980s due to a lack of support). The branch now gives a strong 'Commonwealth' feel to its activities, with branch functions at Canadian, South African, British, New Zealand and Australian consular residences. There is also regular cooperation with different organisations and the other Loyal Societies. The committee includes French, Indian, German, American, Chinese and many other nationals. Many distinguished local people are branch patrons.

From the beginning the Hong Kong branch has concentrated on arranging fund-raising functions to aid local and Commonwealth charities including Riding for the Disabled (fund-raising bought them a horse!), Save the Children, the Hong Kong Ballet and the Hong Kong Federation for the Blind.

The social programme is very active, with the largest function in recent years being the Golden Jubilee Garden Party attended by a thousand people in aid of charity, at which their Royal Highnesses the Earl and Countess of Wessex were present.

New Zealand

Although the ROSL was well established in New Zealand before the war, it was after the return of New Zealand's Second World War servicemen that membership flourished. Many had experienced great hospitality at the ROSL HQ in London and were keen to support the ideals and aims of fostering international friendship and understanding, with membership reaching 6,000 during the 1950s.

Today branches are active in Auckland, Tauranga, Manawatu, Christchurch , Timaru, Oamaru and Southland, with regular monthly meetings involving local speakers. Young musicians perform regularly and are encouraged and supported by members. Commonwealth Day church services and dinners, along with Christmas celebrations, are also highlights of the year.

More recently they have established a Chamber Ensemble Scholarship with sponsorship from Professor Barrie Pettman and Maureen Pettman. Combined with ROSL ARTS a four-day workshop is held for ten ensembles from New Zealand universities. The scholarship offers a five-week residency in the UK with performances, tuition, auditions and attending concerts and festivals. This was won in 2006 by the Antipodes Quartet, in 2007 by Trio Scintillatum and in 2008 by the Duo Giocoso.

It was a great honour for ROSL NZ to hold a concert in 2007 for members around the country at Government House, with visiting ROSL gold-medallists Timothy Orpen, John Myerscough and Alasdair Beatson performing. This was hosted by the New Zealand patron, the Governor-General H.E. Sir Anand Satyanand and Lady Susan Satyanand. In 2009 a concert was held at the New Zealand Parliament building as a joint celebration of the ROSL centenary and the 60th anniversary of Chamber Music New Zealand. The performers were ROSL prizewinners the Barbirolli Quartet.

Switzerland

The first event for members living in Switzerland was held at the Lausanne Hotel School in 1992 during the time when the Director General, Robert Newell, was a visiting lecturer. Mrs Jo Brown, then Honorary Corresponding Secretary in Switzerland, formed the branch in 1993 and became its first chairman. Since then the annual dinners have been held at the hotel school to which leading personalities have been invited as speakers. Membership has consistently been in excess of 250.

Thailand

The Thailand branch, founded in 2006, has been responsible for two significant initiatives to support young Thai musicians and artists in the last few years, aiming to nurture the quality and diversity of young Thai talent to take advantage of the opportunities provided by the League.

This has proved an outstanding success. The Young Musicians of Thailand Competition, held in partnership with the Conrad Hotel, provides a showcase for young people up to the age of 20 to perform in competition in front of 300 invited guests, with the winner having the chance to perform in London. The Young Thai

Artist Competition gives young people the opportunity to compete in exhibiting their work in a two-day exhibition at Siam Pagoda, Bangkok, which attracts many thousands of visitors. The finals, comprising the 12 best works, are held at a gala reception where distinguished international judges select the winner.

Commonwealth Day has been celebrated in recent years in the gardens of the British Embassy, Bangkok, with a sunset garden party.

Honorary Corresponding Secretaries

Honorary Corresponding Secretaries have played a very important part in the life of the League. They were essential in the days before modern communications, providing reliable advice and help for members travelling in their area, and also, hopefully, an enthusiast on the ground to spread the word about the League and encourage others to join.

The wide range of countries and remote regions in which they could be found is demonstrated in the records from 1917 onwards. No doubt the amalgamation of the Over-Seas Club with the Patriotic League of Britons Overseas in 1918 provided many contacts from the latter organisation who were widely scattered and willing to become outposts for the OSL.

In the 1930s annual conferences of HCSs were held at Over-Seas House, London, and Over-Seas House, Edinburgh. These were well attended and provided an opportunity to reinforce League ideals and prospects.

There have been many notable examples of HCSs using their initiatives to create opportunities for League projects, such as the one in Namibia, where HCS Dick Chamberlain has been a strong factor in promoting educational sponsorship.

With the advent of better communications, particularly the Internet, the need for more HCSs has declined. After 2005 no new ones have been created. However, the ROSL still has representatives who make a significant contribution to the League in 60 countries.

The Honorary Corresponding Secretaries world conference in 1934.

Reciprocal Clubs

There has been a long tradition of reciprocation with clubs in the Commonwealth and now throughout the world. This has most commonly come about through need and recommendations from overseas members of the League, followed by appropriate enquiries and approval by the Director General, depending on certain criteria. The clubs should preferably have accommodation and where possible should be mutual societies. There should be no discrimination of any kind in operation, for instance in the case of women travelling alone.

Good examples of the excellent arrangements the ROSL provides with reciprocal clubs are the Tanglin Club and Singapore Cricket Club in Singapore, and the Royal Automobile Club, Victoria, in Australia.

When in Singapore, for example, members can enjoy a choice of restaurants and bars at the Cricket Club (founded in 1852) along with a wide variety of sporting activities including cricket and use of a gym. Although the Cricket Club does not offer bedroom accommodation this can be found in the colonial-style buildings of the Tanglin Club (founded in 1865), which also offers use of a pool and a variety of social pastimes, cultural events and sporting activities.

The Royal Automobile Club, Victoria, as another example, was formed in 1903 and consists of five clubs and resorts. The various sites offer luxurious accommodation, dining facilities, heated swimming pools, golf courses, walking trails, tennis courts and landscaped gardens, amongst other things. It is obvious that reciprocal arrangements can bring benefits to League members and the members of these other clubs.

Reciprocal clubs: Singapore Cricket Club.

Reciprocal clubs: Royal Automobile Club Victoria, Melbourne.

The Return of the Missing Picture

In the 1980s a picture by George Harcourt of King George VI and his family which hung in the Willingdon Drawing Room at Over-Seas House was inadvertently sold to Peter Langan, the former restaurateur who owned Langan's Brasserie in London at the time.

Some years later when Robert Newell became Director-General, he was determined to buy the picture back from Peter Langan's widow, Susan. Curiously enough, the picture had been missing after the closure of the Langans' Los Angeles restaurant where it had been among many pictures adorning the walls. All the pictures had been returned from the USA except the one in question. After further investigations in LA, the picture was found languishing in Hollywood. At Robert Newell's instigation, the picture was flown back, purchased from Mrs Langan, and within seven days of its arrival was reinstated in its original position. Thanks to Peter Langan's restoration of the work, the picture looked better than ever and members were delighted to have it restored to them.

A Near Miss

On 27 September 1990 the IRA endeavoured to cause a major explosion in the conference room at Over-Seas House, London, in what was then called St Andrew's Hall, now Princess Alexandra Hall. A bomb was placed under the lid of the lectern on the eve of a conference on terrorism at which the then Commissioner of the Metropolitan Police, Sir Peter (now Lord) Imbert, and a Government Minister, William Waldegrave, were to be the speakers, who were targets along with the conference. Thankfully, due to the diligence of Conference and Banqueting Manager Tony Hanmer, the bomb was discovered and defused in time. Newspapers throughout the world carried reports of this incident and the then General Manager, Robert Newell, was interviewed by broadcasting companies, which resulted in a significant surge in membership applications over the following months.

Concert at Lancaster House

In 1992 the League held a particularly memorable concert at Lancaster House, in conjunction with the Commonwealth Foundation, to mark the 40th anniversary of both The Queen's accession and the ROSL Music Competition.

This was a spectacular event, with ethnic musicians being brought from all over the world through the auspices of the Commonwealth Music Association, including Inuit Throat Singers from Cape Dorset, Canada, and musicians from Tonga, the Gambia, Malaysia and the Solomon Islands, and Caribbean, and folk musicians from Barbados and Trinidad and Tobago. The range of performers was extraordinary – never before had such vastly differing styles been brought together in this way. This would not have been possible without the support of a large number of sponsors who covered the cost of flights and accommodation for the musicians.

Roderick Lakin, the League's director of Arts, devised an imaginative programme. The world of classical music was represented by young winners of the ROSL Music Competition whose performances both blended and contrasted with the enormous variety of ethnic music. At the end of the concert each musician had the honour of being presented to HM The Queen, who was familiar with much of their music from her extensive royal tours. Sightsavers (the Royal Commonwealth Society for the Blind) benefited from the proceeds of the concert.

Over-Seas House, London and Edinburgh, Architecture and History

A t one time or another the League has had premises through-out the Commonwealth (in 1937 in 30 cities), usually leased and of varied interest and distinction. They have been im-portant to the branches they served as representative outposts of the ROSL and centres of branch activity. However, there has always been an emphasis on the London HQ as the focal point, described by Sir Evelyn Wrench as 'the dynamo ... the generator of energy for the work of our organisation'.[1]

Although the League declared its idealistic aims to be a 'broth-erhood of service' rather than a club, the task of providing good premises for members from all over the world was an obvious pri-ority. The League's growth depended upon it, not only for the fa-cilities provided, but to further its 'aims ... promotion of activities, two-way exchange of goods, services and people'.[2]

Over-Seas House, Park Place, St. James's

The purchase of Vernon House as the Over-Seas HQ in 1921, fol-lowed by other buildings in Park Place and, above all, the beautiful

Rutland House next door in 1934, established the League in St James's. Although Rutland House with its cobbled yard and gatehouse was entered from Arlington Street, it was decided to keep the existing entrance to Over-Seas House and to join Vernon House and Rutland House internally for practical purposes. The addition in 1937 of the Westminster Wing, providing many bedrooms and two lecture halls, was made possible by the destruction of the ballroom of Rutland House and building over its courtyard – unthinkable today under listed building regulations.

Over-Seas House in London is thus essentially an amalgam of two historic houses of eighteenth-century origin plus a 1937 wing. The acquisition of these buildings and their development has provided the ROSL with a fascinating and distinguished building in a prime location in St James's with a garden overlooking Green Park.

St James's itself is one of the most prestigious areas of London. Like much of the so-called 'West End' and the City of Westminster, it was not developed as a fashionable district until after the restoration of King Charles II in 1660, and particularly after the Great Fire of London in 1666. Until that time aristocratic families had lived in or close to the City of London, often along the Strand, in large houses whose gardens stretched down to the River Thames. The move westwards to the rural parts of the ancient city of Westminster was a natural result of the devastation and rebuilding after the fire. The area around the Court at St James's Palace provided undeveloped land ready to be laid out in elegant streets and closes where courtiers could make their homes. The King, always a generous friend, had already granted large tracts of land to his favourites, with the Earl of Arlington, Henry Jermyn and Barbara Castlemaine among others receiving land on both sides of St James's Street.

Park Place was laid out in 1683. Old maps show the intense building spree that took place during the remainder of the century and beyond. Whilst at first occupied exclusively by the nobility such as Lord Clifford and the Countess of Tankeville, after the end of the century a mixture of the houses of the aristocracy and premises catering for their needs such as clubs, gambling dens and brothels existed side by side, as a list of early residents shows. One of the first such in Park Place was that of Mother Needham, a notorious brothel-keeper who kept a house of 'civility' on the site of the later Vernon House. Famously described by Hogarth as a 'handsome old Procuress' and mentioned by Pope in *The Dunciad*,[3] she had a long tenure due to rich protectors and was only convicted of keeping a disorderly house in 1731. Her punishment – standing in the pillory 'over against Park Place' – was slightly mitigated when she was allowed to lie down on her face. However she was 'so severely pelted by the Mobb, that her life was despaired of'.[4] She died later the same year.

The eighteenth century also saw the celebrated Betty, Queen of the Apple-Women, who kept a fruit shop on the corner of St James's Street and Park Place. She is frequently mentioned in Horace Walpole's letters as a convivial woman who went to Vauxhall Pleasure Gardens with parties to whom she supplied her hampers of fruit. More conventional residents were William Pitt and David Hume, and Charles James Fox, who lived in an apartment at 2 Park Place, convenient for Brook's Club next door where he could indulge his passion for gambling. Arlington Street, adjoining Park Place, quickly became popular with government ministers, including Sir Robert Walpole (1716–45).

What is considered Georgian architecture began to develop from 1714 when George I came to the throne. The district of St James's quickly demonstrated the new classical style in beautiful buildings whose main influence was that of Palladio (1508–80), the Italian architect. His buildings of light, space and proportion had been seen by many aristocrats on the Grand Tour. Books of his architectural drawings, made in the sixteenth century, were circulated in England two centuries later, showing how to relate everything in a house 'to the human Frame, creating simple splendour'.[5] It was on these principles that James Gibbs created Rutland House for the Duchess of Norfolk between 1734 and 1740. It was the

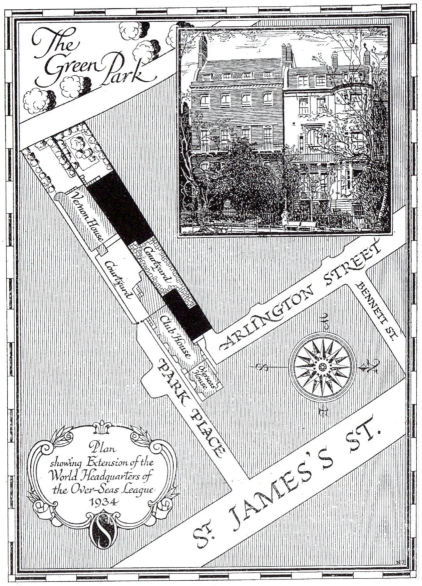

The Green Park

Vernon House

Courtyard

Courtyard

Courtyard

Club House

Overseas House

PARK PLACE

ARLINGTON STREET

BENNETT ST.

ST. JAMES'S ST.

Plan
showing Extension of the
World Headquarters of
the Over-Seas League
1934

Map of Park Place, St James's, from *Overseas*, May 1934.

last London house he designed, a comparatively small building, of three floors overlooking Green Park. It was entered from Arlington Street via a Gatehouse (which can still be seen), an original feature which became fashionable making 'the buildings more retired and quiet' (according to the eighteenth-century *Grub Street Journal*). It was later the home of Lord North.

The house passed into the Rutland family after 1816. George IV's brother and heir Frederick, Duke of York, was a friend of the Duke and particularly the Duchess of Rutland. He spent much time in their home, now known as Rutland House. It was here that he died in his chair in what is now the cocktail lounge, pursued by his creditors to the last and with his new palace next to St James's Palace (now Lancaster House) still being built down the road.

The eighth Duke of Rutland brought his family to live in Rutland House, 16 Arlington Street, in 1898. The best description of the house at the time comes from the memoirs of Lady Diana Cooper (née Manners) the youngest daughter of the famiiy: 'One of the most unspoilt eighteenth-century houses in London', it was 'a huge house boasting electric light and two bathrooms'.[6] The front entrance was through the lodge on Arlington Street and across a cobbled court yard to the main door into a dark hall with the beautiful staircase beyond. Beneath the lodge were 'vast kitchens' and an underground passage by which tradesmen (and all meals) made the long journey to the basement of the main house. Here was the servants' hall and a large room (once the Ulster Room and now ROSL ARTS and PR departments) where the unplaced tomb of Haddon, Lady Diana's brother, sculpted by his mother, stood. Narrow back stairs, known as the Crinoline, went up three flights to the attics, which were reached by wooden stairs.

On the courtyard level was a 'Kent decorated dining room and a library' for the Duke, overlooking Green Park, with an outside staircase to a 'mangy garden'. The Duchess had a sitting room on the courtyard side. On the first floor was a 'vast ballroom' used as a studio, music and play room, facing the courtyard, and a 'gilded Drawing room', which together with the Duchess's bedroom and tiny bathroom (now a cupboard) faced the park. Above were more floors of bedrooms, nurseries and servants' rooms.

Designs for the exterior and interior of Rutland House
by James Gibbs .

An early design for the Gatehouse in Arlington Street.

The house was used as a private hospital during the 1914–18 war. Later, after the Duke's death in 1928, the Duchess moved to the lodge, the house having been 'denuded by a sale' and was in the market waiting for 'some modern Croesus'. The modern Croesus in the form of the Over-Seas League bought the house from the Duchess in 1934. The transformation that took place to meet the League's needs is described by Lady Diana as having '[the] exquisite proportions half obliterated and totally deformed by the Over-Seas League, which has suppressed the William Kent decorations, torn up and roofed over the eighteenth-century courtyard and built a lot of new rooms'.

Although the ballroom was destroyed and much of the interior altered by the ROSL for its purposes, some outstanding features of Gibbs's work still remain, in particular the main staircase from the Central Lounge. This beautiful stair with a balustrade created of wrought iron, then a new building material, connects the two principal floors. The secondary staircase called the Crinoline is a hooped spindle stair, so shaped to allow women in hooped dresses to descend easily from the bedroom floors. The back stair also accommodated the letter carrier operated by a handle, which still survives, which brought letters from the upper floors down to be collected for the post by a uniformed page.

The three first-floor rooms of Rutland House, now known as the Wrench, Rutland and Bennet Clark rooms, contain some fine original work by William Kent in dadoes, carved fireplaces, windows and shutters. The large marble fireplace in the Rutland Room was carved by John Rysbrack, the well-known sculptor who worked frequently with James Gibbs.

Vernon House too had its origin in the eighteenth century, named after Admiral Edward Vernon (1684–1757) whose family lived there. He was the Admiral nicknamed Old Grog, after the shabby Grogram coat he wore habitually, whose prescription of a daily ration of 8oz of 80 per cent water and 20 per cent rum per man was adopted by the Navy to contain and reduce the terrible drunkenness prevalent at the time. The house was entirely rebuilt in 1835 and again, after a fire, in 1905, by Lord Hillingdon who gutted the interior, refurbishing it in the lavish Edwardian style then fashionable. The panelled interiors of the Hall, the Vernon Staircase, Mountbatten Room and Hillingdon Drawing Room all demonstrate the decoration and style of the period.

The two houses combined have given the League beautiful rooms whose use has changed with the demands of the times. The Buttery, for example, originally the restaurant, became the main office until the 1980s, dealing with members and all related activities. The addition of the Westminster Wing in 1937 provided the two large halls, originally intended as a lecture hall and an Empire newspaper room and library, together with the necessary bedrooms. In 1935 Evelyn Wrench referred to the collection of six buildings on the site as 'an Empire Centre'. Funds for the decoration of the main halls came from an appeal to the members, being given appropriate acknowledgement in the chosen name, for example the Hall of India and Pakistan supported by Indian members (including a number of ruling princes) and the former St Andrew's Hall supported by some Scottish members. St Andrew's Hall was renovated to concert standard in 2005 for music events and renamed Princess Alexandra Hall after a further appeal.

The bomb damage in the Second World War to Vernon House and the difficult time that followed led to the League leasing some accommodation locally. During the post-war period too the buildings in Park Place (number 3, freehold, numbers 4 and 5, on lease, and the Gatehouse, freehold) had deteriorated to a dangerous level, with a water-powered lift (with a porter inside) falling two floors, fortunately without serious injury. In 1980, when Peter de Savory established the St James's Club opposite the Park Place buildings and offered to buy both leases and freehold, the Central Council, under Lord Grey, realised that the proceeds of the sale would provide for the complete renovation of Over-Seas House, and simultaneously cancel all the League's outstanding debts.

The destruction of part of Rutland House to make way for the new
Westminster Wing, 1935 . The view from the Gate House in Arlington Street.

SKETCH OF NEW BUILDING, OVERLOOKING THE COURTYARD OF VERNON HOUSE
It is hoped to begin building in March

'Our wonderful new building': design for the 1937 wing.

The League was thus enabled to launch Project 1981 under the direction of a new general manager, Robert Newell, later director general. Not only was there to be a total renovation of the premises, but space had to be found to accommodate the facilities lost in the sale of Park Place – the Victoria bar, buttery, bedrooms, staff accommodation and the men's reading and TV room. This ambitious project, transforming the interior of the building and the kitchen and essential services, was entirely successful and with the addition of extra bathrooms in both the Park and Westminster Wing brought the club facilities up to an unprecedented standard.

The need for more bedroom accommodation was satisfied in 1987 by the addition of a fifth floor on the Westminster Wing, to be followed by a sixth floor in 2003.

In 2004 the Central Council took the radical decision, on the advice of the Director-General, to outsource all food and beverage

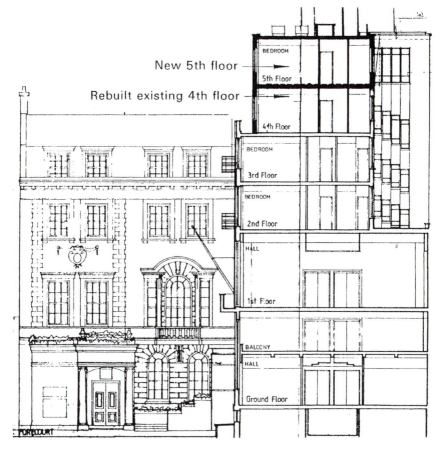

New 5th floor

Rebuilt existing 4th floor

BEDROOM
5th Floor

4th Floor

BEDROOM
3rd Floor

BEDROOM
2nd Floor

HALL
1st Floor

BALCONY
HALL
Ground Floor

FORECOURT

Plan showing the location of the improved bedrooms
on the fourth floor.

catering at Over-Seas House to Convex Leisure Ltd, due to a decline in standards and surpluses. The result has been a significant reduction in overhead costs and an increase in revenue. Convex Leisure has become an associate employer and part of the League family.

The task of maintaining a historic house in central London with all the problems of piping, drainage and subsidence (due to new tube line construction) that this has entailed, whilst creating the most modern standards of comfort, has been accomplished under the guidance of the former house architect Geoffrey Allen, and the Director General.

Geoffrey Allen's records of the state and use of the buildings over the years are a fascinating account of the struggle between conservation and innovation, and above all the need to keep the premises open and working day-to-day whatever the circumstances. Allen also made a study of the historic origins of the buildings, which is invaluable.

Like much else about the ROSL, Over-Seas House unifies past and present in its architecture and facilities, in a harmonious combination.

Over-Seas House, 100 Princes Street, Edinburgh

There has been an Over-Seas Club in Edinburgh for almost as long as the one in St James's, London. The first premises were established in Charlotte Street in the New Town in 1927. Soon outgrown, the League bought 100 Princes Street, a former hotel, in 1929. In order to oversee the necessary renovations, and to initiate a drive to increase membership and promote the club generally, Winifride Wrench, Evelyn Wrench's sister, spent a year in Edinburgh. During that time membership increased to 1,500 local members and in 1930 the new club premises were opened by the Duke of York. It was the first mixed club in the city and boasted 20 bedrooms, a bar and restaurant and other club facilities. All the furnishings were produced and made in Scotland.

The building, formerly the Windsor Hotel, a temperance establishment, had been designed in 1879 by Robert Patterson, part of the rash of Victorian building along Princes Street. Although not particularly distinguished architecturally, 100 Princes Street occupies a wonderful site, directly opposite Princes Street Gardens and the Castle above.

This site was also of interest historically, with an earlier building being occupied by Lady Clerk of Penicuik, a Jacobite hostess and supporter, whose wearing of the White Cockade proclaimed her loyalty to Prince Charles Edward. The house had been visited by many members of the Scottish Enlightenment in the eighteenth century and early nineteenth century.

From 1930 onwards the Club became a popular centre for Commonwealth visitors, with the prime ministers of Canada, Australia and New Zealand all staying there in that year. Perhaps because of the Scottish origins of so many Commonwealth members, the League in Scotland developed rapidly. In 1933 there were 21 centres (branches) and Glasgow as well as Edinburgh had premises. Throughout the 1920s and 1930s membership increased, reaching 6,206 in 1941. The Scottish clubs and branches were very active during the Second World War, providing a great deal of hospitality to overseas troops.

The Club has always been popular with visitors and Scottish members, becoming particularly important after the closure of the Glasgow premises in 1966. Rebuilding plans for the Edinburgh Club began in 1972 as a result of an initiative by Boots the Chemist, which bought part of the old building, demolishing it and occupying the ground floor of the new building while leasing the upper floors back to the League to provide for a new much larger restaurant, bar and enhanced bedroom accommodation. The new wing was opened by the Duke of Gloucester in 1975.

Since 1993 new arts and social programmes for members, plus constant renovation and upgrading of facilities, have brought in new groups and members. 'Fringe' drama groups had used the

Over-Seas House, Edinburgh, from Princes Street.

Princess Alexandra visiting the Edinburgh Club in 1985.

rooms frequently during the Edinburgh Festival, but a decision by James Wilkie, Development Officer, Scotland, and Alan Chalmers, the Edinburgh Clubhouse Manager, and the ROSL Director of Arts Roderick Lakin, to move from drama to music has resulted in a programme of excellent concerts in the club during the Festival, to augment the regular 'Music with a View' concerts and arts lunches that attract many notable speakers. At the millennium Sir Kenneth Scott, James Wilkie and Alan Chalmers established a Commonwealth Week in the City, raising the League's profile. In the inaugural year of the Scottish Parliament a musical evening was held there with performances by young ROSL musicians, which has since become an annual feature. Membership in Scotland is around 1,000, with 650 Edinburgh and district members. There continues to be strong support for all activities from the Glasgow branch.

The Princess Alexandra Hall Project

On 25 January 2006 Princess Alexandra opened the newly refurnished concert hall at Over-Seas House, named in her honour as Vice Patron of the League since 1979.

This hall, part of the Westminster Wing, built in 1937 to complete Evelyn Wrench's 'Empire Centre' at Over-Seas House, had originally been designated the St Andrew's Hall, with funding coming partly from Scottish members of the League, designed together with the Hall of India on the floor above, for lectures, meetings, concerts and conferences. The St Andrew's Lecture Hall was the scene of the Opening Ceremony of the Empire Centre performed on 14 April 1937 by the Duke of Gloucester. To mark the occasion, the first all-Empire radio/telephone ceremony took place linking the audience in London with the Viceroy of India and the Governor-Generals of Canada from Ottawa, of Australia, from Melbourne, and of South Africa, from Pretoria. The link to the Governor-General of New Zealand failed. Sir Evelyn in his speech drew a parallel with the material benefits of the new telephone links and the idealistic good service and citizenship links provided by the ROSL to all members of the Empire.

After this splendid start, St Andrew's Hall continued to be used widely for all kinds of functions. In 1947 the League's Music Circle began a recital series there, under the banner of the Festival of Commonwealth Youth, which was the origin of the present Music Competition.

As the annual Music Festival (renamed the Competition in 1985) grew in importance, the final concert moved from Over-Seas House, first to the Wigmore Hall and then to The Queen Elizabeth Hall. However, all Music Competition auditions and many prize-winners recitals continued to be held at St Andrew's Hall. The hall was not designed originally as a concert auditorium, its limited stage being unable to accommodate a chamber music group and being suitable only for solo or duo performances. Additionally, the refurbishment of the room in the 1950s and 1960s with carpets and curtains deadened the acoustics considerably. The addition of a balcony and upper corridor spoilt the symmetry of the original design.

In 1999 the ROSL ARTS Sponsorship Committee was formed to raise money for a project to transform the hall, for which the prime function would be the performance of chamber music. A brief was drawn up and a number of architects were asked to submit plans. The brief specified the creation of a suitable stage, lighting and flexible seating as well as the technical facilities to allow for a variety of other uses such as conferences and receptions.

Avery Associate Architects, which had won significant awards for its work in transforming facilities at the Royal Academy of Dramatic Art (RADA), was chosen. They produced a design, addressing all aspects of the brief as well as re-creating the elegant style of the original 1930s building. The balcony was removed, together with all extraneous furnishings. The main construction work began in July 2005 and was completed by the end of September when the hall was back in use. The rest of the work, the installation of the curved stage end wall and stage lighting and the upgrading of the foyer, was carried out between October 2005 and January 2006.

An appeal to meet the costs of the refurbishment was launched in 2002 to mark the 50th anniversary of the ROSL Music Competition. The target of £300,000 was met within three years, mainly from members of the League, a success parallel with the creation of the original hall and a tribute to members' recognition of the important part that music and the arts in general have played in the League's history and the greater role they will play in the future.

*The Chairman, Mr Stanley Martin, welcomes Princess Alexandra
at the concert, in January 2006, to mark the reopening of the
concert hall at Over-Seas House, London, and its renaming
as Princess Alexandra Hall in her honour.*

ROSL ARTS

O f all the many enterprises undertaken by the League from the 1920s onwards, the most enduring has been the promotion and fostering of the arts in the support given to young Commonwealth musicians, artists and writers. Initially music was the principal focus, but later a visual arts and literature programme was developed with great success, fulfilling the League's commitment to promote and unite in friendship young artists and musicians from the overseas Commonwealth and the UK.

Concerts had been held frequently in the early years but it was in 1947 that the very active Music Circle, founded by Jessica, Lady Forres, established a recital series at Over-Seas House under the banner of the Festival of Commonwealth Youth. This provided a showcase for outstanding young musicians from the UK and the overseas Commonwealth. The recitals took place in the Hall of India and Pakistan and St Andrew's Hall and many were broadcast live on the BBC World Service during the 1950s. The Festival became competitive in 1952, in response to the large number of young musicians eager to perform, with a first prize of £10. Joan Kemp Potter,

Left to right: Lady Pamela Mountbatten, Richard Bonynge and Harriet Cohen at the 1951 Festival of Commonwealth Youth.

Jacqueline du Pré, winner of the First Prize in 1961 with Sir Lennox Berkeley.

as the new music organiser, devised the selection process. As the Festival became established the next organiser, Patricia Stammers, successfully approached the Gulbenkian Foundation for support. Its grant of £100 for three years ensured the future of the competition.

Audrey Strange, a retired concert singer, became Director of Music in 1962, and under her professional expertise and dedicated leadership over the next 20 years the Festival grew in strength and stature. She was appointed MBE in 1983. In 1972 the final of the Music Festival moved to the Wigmore Hall, courtesy of the Arts Council, and in 1975, through the generosity of Harry Miller, moved to The Queen Elizabeth Hall where it has been held ever since (except for 2006). Myriam Ponsford, Audrey Strange's assistant, succeeded her in 1982.

Since 1984 the Festival has been directed by Roderick Lakin, subsequently the League's first Director of Arts, who has concentrated on expanding ROSL support of prize-winning

Joan Davies, left, Audrey Strange and Barry Douglas after he won the First Prize in 1979.

Roderick Lakin, Director of Arts, receiving a Herald Angel award at the 2007 Edinburgh Festival for the ROSL ARTS Fringe concert series, 'Music at 100 Princes Street'.

musicians outside the Festival itself and on developing an international scholarship programme. He was appointed MBE in 2004 and received an honorary degree from the Royal Academy of Music in 2007.

Over the past 50 years the scope and prestige of the Festival, renamed in 1985 the ROSL Annual Music Competition, has grown immeasurably. By 2010, awards for solo performers, accompanists and chamber ensembles totalled in excess of £55,000. ROSL ARTS also supports prizewinners by sponsoring concert appearances at major venues and festivals throughout the Commonwealth, and by providing promotional materials such as publicity photographs and CDs. A sum of £40,000 per annum is also given for scholarships to enable Commonwealth musicians to make study visits to the UK.

The League's Vice Patron Princess Alexandra has been a loyal and active supporter of the competition since the 1960s. From the first, it has enjoyed the support of eminent musicians as adjudicators. These have included Dame Myra Hess, Sir Malcolm Sargent, Ralph Vaughan Williams, Sir Arnold Bax, Carl Dolmetsch and Leon Goossens. From 1960 to 1979, the chairman of adjudicators was the concert pianist and teacher Joan Davies, who was succeeded by Dame Eva Turner. From 1985 to 2002 the Chairman was Lady Barbirolli. Ian Partridge, Michael Gough Matthews and Gavin Henderson have succeeded her in this position.

Past ROSL prizewinners comprise an impressive group of musicians of the highest calibre who have established prominent careers in most areas of the music profession. Gold medallists include pianists Geoffrey Parsons (1953), John Lill (1963), Melvyn Tan (1976), Barry Douglas (1979), Piers Lane (1982) and Paul Lewis (1992); singers Jean Rigby (1981), Susan Chilcott (1986), Janice Watson (1987), Jonathan Lemalu (2000) and Lucy Crowe (2002); and cellists Jacqueline du Pré (1961) and Liwei Qin (1997). (See Appendix 13, pp.159–67 for a list of major prize and scholarship winners.)

Sir David Scott watches while Princess Alexandra, ROSL Vice-Patron,
signs the visitors book on a visit to Over-Seas House, London,
to celebrate the ROSL 75th anniversary.

The gold medal awarded for First Prize in the ROSL
Annual Music Competition.

Singaporean harpsichordist and pianist Melvyn Tan in 1976, the year he won the ROSL Music Competition Gold Medal.

Lucy Crowe, soprano, at the 2002 competition.

In 1984 the ROSL Annual Exhibition was started by the artist Carol Wyatt (ROSL Director of Arts 1984–6): her brief, to match the Music Competition in quality and scope, providing a showcase for young Commonwealth artists. This was the League's first attempt at an exhibition of professional standard, building on earlier art exhibitions and competitions of a different type both at home and overseas. The new exhibition included up to 50 artists per year, and brought together work by young British artists such as Tracey Emin, Peter Howson and Tai-Shan Schierenberg, with their overseas Commonwealth contemporaries. Due to this annual exhibition, many overseas artists have been able to show their work in the UK for the first time.

Artist Jane Walker working on her portrait of Sir Lawrence Byford
at ROSL, London.

In 2000, the ROSL Annual Exhibition was restructured as a group show for five Commonwealth artists, one each from Africa, the Americas, Asia, Australasia/South Pacific and Europe. Each artist, selected in collaboration with national arts councils, major gallery directors and prominent visual arts institutions, is awarded a travel scholarship and a month-long studio residency in the UK or a Commonwealth country other than their country of origin.

Throughout the year ROSL ARTS organises solo exhibitions at Over-Seas House in both London and Edinburgh. ROSL ARTS also commissions work from young artists in ceramics and glass (used as prizes in the Music Competition), graphic designers and portrait artists. (A selective list of artists supported by ROSL ARTS is given in Appendix 14, pp.174–84.)

The third dimension to the arts programme is that of literature. A popular series of literary lectures and book events was established in 1982, originally in collaboration with the National Book League, with the energetic support of its then director Martyn Goff. Now organised entirely by ROSL ARTS, book events take place throughout the year at Over-Seas House, London, involving a wide range of writers, novelists, biographers, historians, poets and travel writers,

A ceramic trophy by Stephen Dixon created for the 1987
Music Competition.

including such authors as Margaret Atwood, Beryl Bainbridge, Penelope Fitzgerald, Doris Lessing and Ben Okri. The League was also a co-founder in 1987 with the Commonwealth Foundation and Book Trust of the Commonwealth Writers' Prize. Since 2000 the League has supported the Caine Prize for African Literature, providing accommodation for shortlisted authors.

Roderick Lakin as Director of Arts is responsible for an ever-increasing programme of international events in the three spheres of music, arts and literature. To support this ambitious programme, the 'Friends of ROSL ARTS' was created in 1999 to encourage new support, develop audiences and foster the active involvement of arts donors with the League's work. The 'Friends' programme, providing special events and privileges, including cultural trips, garden parties and priority bookings, is a positive point of this initiative.

With the impetus of an active sponsorship committee, under the chairmanship of Graham Lockwood, funds raised between 2002 and 2005 from donations, legacies, sponsorship and subscriptions to the 'Friends' contributed to the total refurbishment of what is now Princess Alexandra Hall.

The opening of the newly restored hall by the Princess in January 2006 was a landmark for ROSL ARTS. For over 50 years musicians had struggled during the early auditions of the ROSL Annual Music Competition with an unsuitable environment and unsympathetic acoustics in what was essentially a lecture hall. The Princess returned to the Hall in January 2009 as guest of honour at a dedication concert for a new Steinway concert grand piano, the funds for which were raised in just one year entirely from members' donations, legacies and 'Friends' subscriptions.

Now the acoustics, layout and amenities of the Hall are, in the words of the Director of Arts, 'worthy of the musicians it is our privilege to support'. The ROSL ARTS initiative unites young people worldwide in a shared endeavour in keeping with the idealistic ambition of the founder. It is a most progressive aspect of the life of the League.

VIII

The League Today

Every organisation that survives to its centenary with vitality owes something to its founder. In the case of the Royal Over-Seas League this is particularly true, since Evelyn Wrench dominated more than 30 years of its early life. In the 70 subsequent years it has been the responsibility of others to carry forward his ideas and adapt them to contemporary life in a relevant way.

Evelyn Wrench's great-niece, the author Anne de Courcy, has summed up her impression of him as 'that rare thing, a practical idealist'.[1] This unusual combination laid the foundation for the success of ROSL.

As the ROSL celebrates its centenary year, with the English Speaking Union not far behind, it is instructive to see how the idealistic concepts on which Evelyn Wrench's two creations were founded have shaped their development.

The ROSL, as we have seen, was to be an 'Empire Brotherhood' with a strong emphasis on educational projects, social welfare and support for music and the arts. The ESU in the early years aimed to bring together the two great English speaking peoples of the world, 'the British Empire and North America in democratic unity'[2] with a similar emphasis on education and support for young people.

Education has indeed remained a cornerstone of both organisations, with a steady development of educational exchanges, scholarships and sponsorship within the ESU achieving its modern purpose 'to promote international understanding through the widening use of the English language throughout the world'.[3] A similar emphasis within the League on sponsorship, particularly for young Commonwealth musicians, artists and writers, has fulfilled Evelyn Wrench's educational ideals for the ROSL. The League's goal of 'Empire Brotherhood' has been a constant feature working through the branches, the projects, and the triumphant survival of the League's two club houses as centres of hospitality and meeting places as complete today and infinitely more comfortable than the 'Empire Centre' of 1937.

None of this could have been achieved without the capacity to adapt to change over the years and the ability to find modern interpretations of the original ideals. This, in turn, has been dependent on the judgement and practical skills of the chairmen, councils, directors, staff and volunteers.

Like many organisations, in the first half of the twentieth century the ROSL exemplified a tradition of voluntary service which, while not unique, is more marked in Great Britain and the overseas Commonwealth than in many other countries. Evelyn Wrench himself and Lady des Voeux (later Lady Wrench) served the League in an honorary capacity. While there were always paid staff, the amount of voluntary work undertaken by thousands of members before and during the Second World War was an essential part of the League's success. The post-war world was very different, however. With time and the retirement of Evelyn Wrench, the slow change from voluntary to professional had begun. This coincided in the 1940s and 1950s with very difficult conditions worldwide, making the League's progress problematic.

Fortunately, Evelyn Wrench himself had established in 1912 the practical framework needed to underpin an organisation in the modern world. The chairman and Central Council to which the Secretary, later the Director-General, reported remained in place with additional committees where appropriate. The Central Council has always been composed of men and women with Commonwealth connections either by birth, or through service or business interests. Recent councils have reflected an increasingly wide range of backgrounds and experience. With the retirement of Evelyn Wrench, and the later ending of the tradition of Royal presidents, the role of the Chairman became more important, with the Director-General being a key position needing the necessary vision and skills to steer the League in new directions.

If adaptability to changing conditions has been an essential factor in the League's success, an equally important aspect has been the retention of core values. This has been a matter of fine judgement for recent councils, and particularly for the Director-General as the interpreter of these values in practical terms.

Initially, Evelyn Wrench aimed at a worldwide membership of a million or at least 50,000 and the latter target was last narrowly achieved in the 1960s. Today it is recognised that numbers alone are not the benchmark. It is the quality and diversity of the League's objectives that makes membership attractive. The extension of membership to corporate organisations and, latterly, to non-Commonwealth members, has given the ROSL a broad appeal. The excellent standards of facilities for conferences, receptions and occasions of all kinds mean that an enormous number of people have experience of the League today.

To some extent this has always been the case, but whereas before such experiences might have included coming up from boarding school to have tea with a travelling aunt, it is now far more likely to involve assisting at a concert, conference or competition with people of one's own age and interests. In many respects the membership resembles a modern 'friends' organisation, happily exemplified at Over-Seas House by the contemporary 'Friends of ROSL ARTS'.

The archives of the League and its branches are few – in part due to wartime damage but also perhaps because people have been too busy carrying out the League's practical purposes rather than documenting them. However, the excellent bound editions of *Over-seas* magazine record 94 years of ceaseless activity and the changing prospects and current preoccupations of the League's members.

The ROSL has good reason to celebrate its centenary. The ideals of the founder, his years of dedication, the ability of those who succeeded him, and the enthusiasm and commitment of the membership have created a contemporary organisation with many interesting objectives. There may well be surprising new initiatives to come.

Recent Welfare Projects:
Sri Lanka, Western Australia and Namibia

In the early 1990's the League, as part of its remit to 'give service to the Commonwealth and humanity at large' began to develop small welfare initiatives in partnership with overseas organisations requiring support in kind. The first was the Sri Lanka/ROSL project to support eye care camps for tea plantation workers who lived in the 'lines', in single rooms often shared with poultry.

This came about through a chance meeting between Ashruff Aziz, Chairman of Sri Lanka's Aziz Foundation, which undertook tea plantation welfare work, and Margaret Adrian-Vallance, ROSL's new Director of PR, who had previously worked on development projects in several of the 44 member countries of the Duke of Edinburgh's Award International Association, including Sri Lanka.

Mr Aziz asked if ROSL would put out an appeal for prescription glasses that could be graded by the Colombo Eye Bank, and a team of nurses would then conduct eye tests and match spectacles to requirements. The Aziz Foundation would fund all transport costs including the travel of the PR Director to Sri Lanka to help raise awareness of these health care needs. The appeal that followed collected over 3,000 pairs of spectacles and these were boxed up and free-freighted out to the Colombo Eye Bank by Air Lanka. James Soh, Singapore Youth Award Chairman, then launched 'Operation Vision' and 1,200 more glasses were sent to eye camps in Badulla and Nawalapitiya. Not all were perfect matches but the Eye Bank and villagers considered their improved sight of great benefit.

The second wave of welfare projects also saw a happy liaison with the Duke of Edinburgh's Award, this time in Perth, Western Australia. Here, Award Coordinator Anna Dean, concerned about the difficulties facing isolated youngsters, sought ROSL help for a Youth in Business initiative including a leaflet and a small amount of funding for a wheelchair production centre employing young people. ROSL and the Duke of Edinburgh's Award were further linked when Mrs Dean became ROSL Branch Secretary in 1997.

Both these projects encouraged the start of an important new initiative in 1995. Supported by ROSL's Central Council, Margaret Adrian-Vallance, together with the HCS for Namibia, Dick Chamberlain, members of the Namibian government (Speaker Mose Tjitendero, Minister of Local Government Libertine Amathila and Deputy Minister of Basic Education Clara Bohitile), Air Namibia, the University of Namibia's Vice Chancellor Peter Katjavivi and three primary schools joined in a project to help San (Bushmen) and farm children to gain an education.

At this time Namibia (population only 2 million) faced many challenges. At independence from South Africa in 1990, the country chose English as the national language so most children had to learn this. Large areas were not on the national grid. Some former 'white-only' secondary schools had difficulty adjusting to post-apartheid Namibia. On the big commercial farms with drives of up to 13 miles long farm workers' children had little means of finding a school place, let alone funding one.

Initially an appeal in *Overseas* for books and other items to be free-freighted out by Air Namibia had a great response: a Canberra group ingeniously got an oil tanker to deliver theirs into Walvis Bay; members like Enid Bates involved local schools; branches bought biros and crayons; Dorling Kindersley and writers donated books; inventor Trevor Baylis gave clockwork radios; Banqueting Manager Tony Hanmer raided his stores for candles; and Mairi Radcliffe found T-shirts and sweaters.

This then encouraged more substantial support, with ROSL member Paul Shipman becoming the first financial donor. Clara Bohitile and the Ministry of Education requested that money raised was used to support annual school bursaries covering fees, clothes, books, shoes, hostel accommodation and other necessities.

In 1996 ROSL funded the first nine bursaries for Bushmen and 'farm children' at three primary schools near the Kalahari – Hippo, Mokaleng and Gquina. All had the essential hostel accommodation needed for children from remote areas. As more funds were raised, ROSL was able to extend bursaries to secondary level and then to tertiary level – at Windhoek College of Education and the

Clara Bohitile MP (Namibia), formerly Deputy Minister of Basic Education and Culture.

University of Namibia (UNAM). By 2000 there were ROSL supported schools and individuals in the north, east and west of the country.

By 2007 a pleasing aspect was that several were back in their homelands teaching. One was Cwisa Cwi, the first Bushman to qualify as a teacher, who sometimes joined Margaret as adviser on her annual monitoring visits with Dick Chamberlain, UNAM's

Language Director, or Walter Nel, Chief Inspector of Education. Cwisa enjoyed inspiring others and gaining public speaking experience: 'Not all Bushmen want to be just hunter gatherers,' he said. 'There are many ways of combining modern life with tradition. I will always be grateful to ROSL for helping me this way.'[4]

Cwisa is now Principal of the five bush schools in the Nyae Nyae conservancy where his sister Katrina, also a former ROSL bursary recipient, is a Radio Tsumkwe broadcaster. Three of the first nine in the project, Elias Araeb, Ellie Velskoen and Jon Noadeb, are also teachers, as are later bursary recipients Kaijandere Kaizondjou and Melissa Uses from Himba communities in the north.

Another of the project's highlights has been the progress of the isolated but dedicated Huigub Primary School near Tsumeb. For many years ROSL was the only major donor, funding items from floors to chair repair. In spite of poverty, floods, droughts, food shortages and meningitis, Huigub came fifth out of 137 schools for examination results in 2008. ROSL also donates to the isolated and stoical Katora Primary School in the Namib Desert, as well as supporting individual bursaries there.

The third school ROSL has supported over the years is the remarkable Hippo Primary near Gobabis, which also undertakes pastoral care of its former ROSL youngsters as they progress to secondary or tertiary level. Elrico Slinger, a former pupil, is one of three ROSL bursary recipients to be voted head boy or girl of their secondary school.

Students have remarked often on the importance to them of ROSL interest in their progress and consider this to have been as vital as the financial arm. Clara Bohitile's view of the project is that 'ROSL went that extra mile which is why these kids have succeeded. They fall out of the system because nobody cares. This project keeps them in.'[5]

This welfare project is exactly the sort of scheme, true to the League's idea of providing practical service to the people of the Commonwealth which, established through the dedication of a few people and the sponsorship of many League members, has made a real difference in people's lives.

ROSL bursary recipient Belinda Awases carries one of the renovated chairs back into the classroom at Huigub Primary.

Elias Araeb, ROSL bursary awardee at Hippo Primary, Wennie du Plessis Secondary and Windhoek College of Education with his class at Rakutuka Primary in the Omaheke.

IX

The Royal Over-Seas League and the Future

by the Director General

When I joined the League in October 1979 it lost, in that year, over £100,000 (well over a million pounds today) and the talk at Central Council meetings was about selling the London and Edinburgh premises. The plan was to buy an alternative club house but in the provinces. Well, here we are in 2010, still in the buildings purchased by our founder. Over-Seas House looks better than ever, having been expanded to provide members with accommodation and facilities of five-star standard. Restoration of the historic architecture has been accomplished alongside the installation of the latest technology. And the dire financial situation of the late 1970s, when the very future of the League was in peril, has been replaced by healthy finances in the second millennium.

At the time that the League appeared to be in trouble, so too did the Commonwealth. Its break-up seemed a definite possibility and was predicted by many pundits. The main cause for this pessimism was the row over Britain's refusal to impose sanctions on South Africa during the worst abuses of the apartheid era. But, like the League, the Commonwealth has weathered the storms and is more vibrant and meaningful today than ever under the leadership of its visionary secretary general, Kamalesh Sharma. The Royal Over-Seas League remains loyal to the Commonwealth's aims and ideals and is better placed than ever to help achieve them. Today, the future of the two organisations is assured, with membership of both continuing to expand.

So, what of the future of the League as it enters its second century and I come to the end of my time as its director general and my 30 years with the League? When I assumed the position as chief executive in 1991 I said that I would strive to lead the League into the twenty-first century on a sound financial footing whilst at the same time ensuring that its Royal Charter's aims were achieved and expanded. My principle objectives were to ensure a future with positive cash-flow, an excess of income over expenditure, increased events and activities for members, more overseas branches, an enlarged and more active cultural programme, and further development of the premises in London and Edinburgh. I am proud to say that these goals have been now achieved, with considerable support from my highly competent, enthusiastic and skilled colleagues. They, with my successor, will build on these foundations and work to further expand membership benefits and facilities, and to support the ever important ideals of Commonwealth.

The challenging issues facing the governments of the world and its peoples – rising energy and food costs; depletion of natural resources; population growth; climate change; and economic pressures, to mention just a few – will have a significant impact on the future of the League and they must be confronted with vision and courage. New markets for membership will need to be explored and means to increase revenue must be developed. Further funding of the League's charitable endeavours in the fields of culture and humanitarian projects must be found through donations and legacies. More will need to be done at the club houses to minimise our impact on the environment by reducing waste, recycling, improving energy efficiency and reducing carbon emissions. The League itself will participate in the debate about how to tackle issues that threaten the stability of world communities through, amongst other things, debate in the quarterly journal *Overseas* and at Discussion Group meetings. We will need to play a more proactive role in world affairs, as was the case in the ROSL's early days under the leadership of Evelyn Wrench.

The League must continue to be relevant to the needs of its members in the changing and challenging years ahead and must seek new ways to attract younger members, who may be less emotionally attached to the Commonwealth but have more interest in international affairs. By expanding its cultural endeavours the League will be well positioned to explore Commonwealth issues and ideals with a younger audience and by so doing will help the younger generation, especially in those Commonwealth countries presently ruled by authoritarian and corrupt governments, to influence change and develop good governance in their homelands. The role the League has always played in fostering friendship and understanding amongst people of different races, religions and communities will be more important than ever in the years to come as differences in ethnicity, religion and ideology continue to cause discord amongst international communities.

Nevertheless, as well as such important ideals, which lie at the very heart of everything the League does, the pragmatic benefits that encourage people to join the League must never be neglected. The demand for quality bedroom accommodation has grown substantially over the past two decades and will continue to do so; therefore a means to provide more bedrooms must be identified. Over the next few years the League will need to look into acquiring additional buildings, with access to sports facilities, health spas and exercise centres, which will offer stylish and contemporary facilities suitable to take the League through this century and beyond.

As I step aside and hand the reins of leadership to my successor I look back upon the past 30 years with enormous pleasure. I have made close friendships with many members throughout the world and with many colleagues. I have travelled extensively, both on behalf of the League as well as privately. I have witnessed the formation of new overseas branches; the strengthening finances of the organisation as a whole; improved club house facilities; the expansion of the arts programmes; and above all the ability of the League to adapt to ever-changing political and economic circumstances. I am confident that the sound foundations that are now established will ensure a prosperous and meaningful future for the Royal Over-Seas League as it embarks on its second hundred years.

Robert Newell
Director-General, 1991–

APPENDICES

1. The Royal Over-Seas League Timeline

1882	Birth of founder, Sir Evelyn Wrench
1887	**First Colonial Conference of Empire Premiers held in London**
1898	**Empire Day introduced in Canadian schools by Clementina Trenholme on the last school day before 24 May, Queen Victoria's birthday**
1901	**Death of Queen Victoria**
1904	**Empire Day on 24 May instituted in the UK**
1906	Evelyn Wrench's first vision of his 'Empire Brotherhood' during visit to Canada
1910	Over-Seas Club founded on 27 August by Evelyn Wrench
1911	First public meeting of the 300 members of the Club at the Memorial Hall, Farringdon Street, London EC, on 27 June, the week after the coronation of George V
1912–13	Evelyn Wrench and his sister Winifrede made a 64,000-mile tour of the Empire promoting the Club
1913	Over-Seas Club reorganised with Richard Jebb as the first Chairman and a committee to which Evelyn Wrench reports. Viscount Northcliffe elected President
1914	First premises rented in Aldwych, London
	Outbreak of the First World War in August
1915	Fund-raising for aircraft, comforts for the troops and hospital support began in the Over-Seas Club worldwide and continued throughout the War
	£978,326 raised by 1920
	Overseas magazine created
1916	King George V became first royal patron
1917	Sir Frederick Truby King's 'Babies of the Empire' project began in UK sponsored by the Over-Seas Club
	Evelyn Wrench made CMG for War Services

1918	**First World War ended in November**
	Amalgamation with The Patriotic League of Britons Overseas, becoming Over-Seas League
1922	Vernon House, London SW1, bought as the League's war memorial to Empire troops, and its headquarters, opened by the Duke of York
	League incorporated by Royal Charter. King George V and Queen Mary visited headquarters
	Membership 32,506
1923	61-year lease of 3 Park Place acquired
1924	4 & 5 Park Place, London SW1, bought
1925	Edward, Prince of Wales opened Park Place premises
1927	First Edinburgh premises opened in North Charlotte Street
1930	Scottish headquarters at 100 Princes Street opened by the Duke of York
	1,500 local members
1931	21st Birthday Banquet at the Royal Albert Hall
1932	Evelyn Wrench made Knight Bachelor
1933	Purchase of Rutland House, 16 Arlington Street, next door to Vernon House from Violet, Duchess of Rutland
	Membership 44,555
1937	Empire Centre comprising existing buildings plus new Westminster Wing completed with funds raised entirely by members. Opened by the Duke of Gloucester
	First all-radio telephone link from all parts of the Empire took place at a public function in St Andrew's Hall
	Evelyn Wrench marries Lady des Voeux
1939	**Outbreak of the Second World War in September**
1940	Allies Welcome Committee founded and organised by Sir Jocelyn Lucas to give hospitality and support to all allied troops. Continued with great success until 1950
1940–1	Sir Evelyn and Lady Wrench touring abroad became stranded in India for the duration of the War. Eric Rice took over Evelyn Wrench's duties and subsequently his position as Secretary of the League for the duration of the war

1944   **First Commonwealth Prime Minsters' Conference held in London**

1945   **Allied Victory in Europe and Japan**

Membership 58,261

1946   Air Vice-Marshal Malcolm Henderson became first Director General

King George VI, Queen Elizabeth, Princess Elizabeth and Princess Margaret visited Over-Seas House, London

1947   The Music Circle established a recital series under the banner 'Festival of Commonwealth Youth'

India and Pakistan gained independence within the Commonwealth

1952   The Festival of Commonwealth Youth became competitive. Early winners included Australian pianist Geoffrey Parsons (1953), British cellist Jacqueline du Pré (1961) and British pianist John Lill (1963)

1956   Philip Crawshaw became Secretary General and subsequently Director General

1958   **Empire Day renamed Commonwealth Day, held on the second Monday in March and marked by a multi-faith service in Westminster Abbey**

1959   Earl Mountbatten of Burma President of the League since 1942 becomes its first Grand President

1960   The League has 'Royal' title conferred by HM The Queen on its 50th anniversary

Armorial bearings granted

Sir Evelyn Wrench appointed KCMG

1962   50,000+ members

1966   Death of Sir Evelyn Wrench. Arts Scholarship Fund established in his memory

1967   Membership declines to 38,315

1971   **First biennial Commonwealth Heads of Government Meeting (CHOGM) held in Singapore. Hosted since by different Commonwealth countries in rotation**

1972   Final concert of Festival of Commonwealth Youth moved to London's Wigmore Hall and subsequently to The Queen Elizabeth Hall in 1975

1975	New wing of Over-Seas House, Edinburgh, opened by the Duke of Gloucester
1979	Captain John Rumble RN (rt'd) became Director General. Robert Newell appointed General Manager
1980	Burney Committee discusses amalgamation of the Loyal Societies of the Commonwealth – no agreement reached
	Sale of Park Place properties realises £815,000
1981	Project 81 launched to upgrade Over-Seas House, London
1982	Inauguration of Book Event series at Over-Seas House, London, initially in collaboration with the National Book League (now Book Trust)
1984	ROSL Annual Exhibition for young Commonwealth artists (age limit 35) inaugurated
1985	Festival of Commonwealth Youth renamed ROSL Annual Music Competition
	League's 75th anniversary
1987	Fifth floor of bedrooms added to Westminster Wing, Over-Seas House, London, opened by Countess Moutbatten of Burma
	Commonwealth Writers Prize founded by ROSL, Commonwealth Foundation and the Book Trust
1991	Robert Newell, former General Manager, is appointed Director General
1992	Concert of Music and Musicians of the Commonwealth held at Lancaster House, London, for HM The Queen to mark the 40th anniversary of her accession
1993	ROSL secured official recognition as a Commonwealth non-governmental organisation (NGO) and was represented for the first time at CHOGM in Cyprus
1995	Namibia Welfare and Educational initiative created
1998	ROSL affiliated membership extended to non-Commonwealth citizens
1999	Friends of ROSL ARTS established
2000	ROSL ARTS Commonwealth Visual Arts Travel Scholarships (up to five per annum) inaugurated. ROSL Annual Scholars exhibition replaces ROSL Annual Exhibition
	Membership 21,039

2003	Sixth floor of bedrooms added to Westminster Wing opened by Countess Mounbatten of Burma
2006	Extensive refurbishment of St Andrew's Hall, Over-Seas House, as a concert room. Re-opened by HRH Princess Alexandra and renamed Princess Alexandra Hall in her honour
2009	History of ROSL written by Adele Smith published by I.B.Tauris
2010	ROSL celebrated its centenary. An appeal was launched to endow awards in excess of £50,000 annually in the ROSL Annual Music Competition.
	The Queen and Princess Alexandra agree to attend a reception for members at St James's Palace
	Service of Thanksgiving at St James's Church, Piccadilly. Many other celebratory events held at ROSL branches throughout the world

2. Patrons

1916–36	HM King George V
1936	HM King Edward VIII
1937–52	HM King George VI
1952–	HM Queen Elizabeth II

3. Vice Patrons

1916–42	HRH The Duke of Connaught, KG, KT, KP, GCB, GCSI, GCMG, GCIE, GCVO, GBE
1920–36	HRH The Prince of Wales, KG, KT, KP, GCSI, GCMG, GCIE, GCVO, GBE, ISO, MC (later King Edward VIII and Duke of Windsor)
1942–74	HRH The Duke of Gloucester, KG, KT, KP, GCB, GCMG, GCVO
1946–52	HRH The Princess Elizabeth, Duchess of Edinburgh, Lady of the Garter, CI (later Queen Elizabeth II)
1979–	HRH Princess Alexandra, KG, GCVO

4. Presidents

1916–22	Viscount Northcliffe
1922–36	HRH The Duke of York, KG, KT, KP, GCMG, GCVO (later King George VI)
1937–42	HRH The Duke of Kent, KG, KT, GCMG, GCVO
1942–59	Admiral of the Fleet, The Rt Hon. Earl Mountbatten of Burma, KG, GCB, OM, GCSI, GCIE, GCVO, DSO (Grand President 1959–79)
1962–81	Sir Angus Gillan, KBE, CMG
1981–93	Lord Grey of Naunton, GCMG, GCVO, OBE (Grand President 1993–9)
1998–2002	Sir David Scott, GCMG
2002–	The Rt Hon. Lord Luce, KG, GCVO, DL

5. Chairmen

1913–14	Mr Richard Jebb
1916–18	Mr Willian Bulkeley-Evans, CBE
1922–9	Sir Ernest Birch, KCMG
1929–33	Mr Alec Rea
1933–6	The Rt Hon. Sir John Tilley, GCMG, GCVO, CB
1936–41	The Rt Hon. Viscount Goschen, GCSI, GCIE, CB
1941	The Most Hon. the Marquess of Willingdon, PC, GCSI, GCMG, GCIE, GBE
1941–6	Marie, Marchioness of Willingdon, CI, GBE
1946–9	Sir Shenton Thomas, GCMG, OBE
1949–52	Air Chief Marshal Sir Arthur Longmore, GCB, DSO
1952–5	Sir Henry Craik, GCIE, KCSI
1955–62	Sir Angus Gillan, KBE, CMG
1962–8	Sir James Robertson, KT, GCMG, GCVO, KBE
1968–71	Admiral Sir David Luce, GCB, DSO, OBE
1971–6	Marshal of the RAF Lord Elworthy, KG, GCB, CBE, DSO, LVO, DFC, AFC
1976–81	Lord Grey of Naunton, GCMG, GCVO, OBE
1981–6	Sir David Scott, GCMG
1986–9	Mr Maneck Dalal, OBE
1989–92	Sir Lawrence Byford, CBE, QPM, DL
1992–5	Mr Peter McEntee, CMG, OBE
1995–2000	Sir Geoffrey Ellerton, CMG, MBE
2000–5	Sir Colin Imray, KBE, CMG
2005–9	Mr Stanley Martin, CVO
2009–	Sir Anthony Figgis, KCVO, CMG

6. Secretaries, Secretary-Generals and Director-Generals

1912–42	Sir Evelyn Wrench, KCMG Secretary
1942–6	Mr Eric Rice, OBE Secretary
1946–56	Air Vice Marshal Malcolm Henderson, CB, CIE, CBE, DSO Director-General
1956–9	Mr Philip Crawshaw, CBE Secretary-General
	later
1959–79	Director-General
1979–91	Captain John Rumble, RN (Rtd) Director General
1991–	Mr Robert Newell, LVO Director-General

7. Vice-Presidents
as at January 2010

Their Excellencies the Commonwealth Secretary-General and the
High Commissioners for Commonwealth countries in London
The Viscount Boyd of Merton
Dame Mary Bridges, DBE
Sir Lawrence Byford, CBE, QPM, DL
Mrs Yvonne Calver
The Cardinal Archbishop of Westminster
The Rt Hon. the Baroness Chalker of Wallasey
Mr Colin Clark
Mr Maneck Dalal, OBE
The Dean of Westminster
Mr Martyn Goff, CBE
The Lady Gore-Booth
The Lord Imbert, CVO, QPM
Sir Colin Imray, KBE, CMG
Mr Graham Lockwood
The Lord Chief Justice of England and Wales
Mr Stanley Martin, CVO
Mr Robert Matheson, CM, QC
The Countess Mountbatten of Burma, CBE, CD, JP, DL
Sir David Scott, GCMG
Sir Kenneth Scott, KCVO, CMG
Sir Donald Tebbit, GCMG
The Rt Hon. the Lord Woolf

8. Central Council
as at January 2010

Miss Farah Amin
Mrs Marilyn Archbold* (Deputy Chairman)
Mr Graham Archer, CMG
Mrs Shirley Barr*
Mr Ralph Bauer
Mr Clive Carpenter
Sir Roger Carrick, KCMG, LVO
Mr Christie Cherian*
Nik Raof Daud
Mr Paul Dimond, CMG
Mr John Edwards, CMG*
Mrs Patricia Farrant
Sir Anthony Figgis, KCVO CMG* (Chairman)
Mr Simon Gimson
Ms Diana Gray
Mr Robert Gregor, MBE
Sir James Hodge, KCVO CMG
Mr David Jamieson
Mrs Beryl Keen
Mrs Anne de Lasta
The Rt Hon. Lord Luce, KG GCVO, DL (President)
Miss Sheila MacTaggart, LVO
Dr Edmund Marshall
Mr David Newman
Mr Ian Partridge, CBE
Mrs Doreen Regan*
Mrs Judith Steiner*
Mr Geoffrey Thompson, OBE
Mrs Pamela Voice
Mr Simon Ward, FCA* (Hon. Treasurer)

* Executive Committee

9. Senior Staff
as at January 2010

Mr Robert Newell LVO	Director-General
Mrs Fatima Vaniček	Asst to the Director-General/ Membership Secretary
Mr Roderick Lakin, MBE	Director of ARTS
Miss Margaret Adrian-Vallance	Director of Public Relations and Development
Mr Rachid Mellah	Rooms Division Manager
Mr Shakil Tayub	Director of Finance and Administration
Mr Paul Streat	Maintenance Manager
Mr Michael McCall	Head Hall Porter and Health and Safety Officer
Mrs Deisy Garcia	Head Housekeeper
Mr Abdul Amrani	Purchasing Officer
Mr Alan Chalmers	House Manager, ROSL Edinburgh
Mr James Wilkie	Scottish Development Officer, ROSL Edinburgh
Mr David Anderson	Chef de Cuisine, ROSL Edinburgh
Ms Lena Rose	Head Receptionist, ROSL Edinburgh
Mr David Laurance	Catering Director, Convex Leisure
Mr Tony Hanmer	Conference and Banqueting Manager, Convex Leisure
Mr Losine Khezour	Chef des Cuisine, Convex Leisure

10. ROSL Branches
as at January 2010

UK

BRANCH	*CHAIRMEN*
Bath	Mrs June Jessop
Bournemouth	Mr Christopher Bladen
Cheltenham	Mr John Miller, MBE
Edinburgh	Mr Robert Gregor, MBE
Exeter	Mr Ewan MacLeod
Glasgow	Mr William Agnew
West Cornwall	Mrs Margaret Knighton
West Sussex	Mrs Marilyn Archbold

Overseas

AUSTRALIAN BRANCH

New South Wales	Mrs Lily Murray (Secretary)
Queensland	Mrs Sharon Morgan (Chairman)
South Australia	Mrs Marjorie Scriven (President)
Tasmania	Mr Robert Dick (Chairman)
Victoria	Mr Jason Ronald, OAM (President and ROSL Chairman Australia)
Western Australia	Mr Jeffery Turner, MBE (Chairman)

CANADIAN CHAPTERS	*PRESIDENTS*
Alberta	Mrs Cynthia Cordery
British Columbia	Mrs Pamela Ducommun
Nova Scotia	Mrs Barbara Hughes QC
Ontario	Ms Ishrani Jaikaran

The Royal Over-Seas League

EGYPT BRANCH	Prof Abdallah Schleifer
HONG KONG BRANCH	Mr Paul Surtees (President)
NEW ZEALAND	
Headquarters	Mrs Lyn Milne (ROSL Director New Zealand)
	PRESIDENTS
Auckland	Mrs Val Sullivan
Christchurch	Mrs Judith Leckie
Manawatu	Mrs Helen Thompson (Patron)
Oamaru	Mr Dennis Norman
South Canterbury	Mr Len Home, QSM
Southland	Mrs Eunice Sutton
SAUDI ARABIA BRANCH	Mr John Freel OBE (Chairman)
SWITZERLAND BRANCH	Mrs Jo Brown MBE (Chairman)
THAILAND BRANCH	Mr James Napier (Chairman)

11. Honorary Corresponding Secretaries
as at January 2010

There are HCSs in the following countries, states, counties and towns.

UK

England	Essex, Manchester, Norfolk, Oxford
Scotland	Aberdeen, Blairgowrie, Inverness, Moffat, Perth
Ireland	Belfast, County Down
Wales	Haverford West

Overseas

Arabian Gulf	Doha, Qatar
Australia	Adelaide, Kincumber, New South Wales, Perth, Queensland, Tasmania, Victoria, Viewmont
Bahrain	Adliya, Manama
Belgium	Ways-la-Hutte
Bermuda	Paget, Warwick
Botswana	Gaborone
Brazil	Rio de Janeiro
Canada	Alberta, British Columbia, Newfoundland, Nova Scotia, Ontario
China	Beijing
Colombia	Bogotá
Cyprus	Nicosia
Egypt	Cairo
France	Loire Valley
Germany	Berlin, Frankfurt, Hamburg, Köln/Düsseldorf, Malente-Benz

Ghana	Sekondi
Gibraltar	
Hong Kong	
Iceland	Reykajavik
India	Kolkata, Chenai, Mumbai, New Delhi, Pune
Italy	Florence, Milan
Kenya	Malindi, Nairobi
Malta	Sliema, Valletta
Mauritius	Quatre Bournes
Nigeria	Kaduna
New Zealand	Hamilton, Auckland
Portugal	Lisbon
Saudi Arabia	Riyadh
South Africa	Cape Town, Knysna, Pietermaritzburg
Spain	Malaga
Sweden	Gothenburg
Switzerland	
Tanzania	Dar es Salaam
Thailand	Bangkok
USA	Atlanta, Connecticut, Florida, Massachusetts, Minnesota, Seattle

12. Reciprocal Clubs
as at January 2010

Australia
Brisbane Polo Club, Brisbane, Queensland
Karrakatta Club Inc., Perth
New South Wales Masonic Club, Sydney, New South Wales
North Queensland Club, Townsville, Queensland
RACV City Club, Melbourne, Victoria
RACV Cobram Resort, Cobram, Victoria
RACV Healesville Resort, Healesville, Victoria
RACV Inverloch Resort, Victoria
Royal Automobile Club of Australia, Sydney, New South Wales
Tattersall's Club, Brisbane, Queensland
University House, Canberra

Brunei
Royal Brunei Yacht Club, Brunei Darussalam

Canada
Edmonton Petroleum Club and Golf and Country Club, Edmonton, Alberta
Glencoe Club, Calgary, Alberta
Halifax Club, Halifax, Nova Scotia
Mount Stephen Club, Montreal, Quebec
Ranchmen's Club, Calgary, Alberta
Royal Canadian Military Institute, Toronto, Ontario
Royal Glenora Club, Edmonton, Alberta
Royal Nova Scotia Yacht Squadron, Halifax, Nova Scotia
Royal Victoria Yacht Club, Victoria, British Columbia
Terminal City Club, Vancouver, British Columbia
University Club of Toronto, Toronto, Ontario

The Royal Over-Seas League

Canary Islands
British Club, Las Palmas

Channel Islands
Victoria Club, St Helier, Jersey

England
City University Club, London

Gibraltar
Royal Gibraltar Yacht Club, Gibraltar

Hong Kong
Hong Kong Cricket Club, Hong Kong

India
Bangalore Club, Bengaluru
Bengal Club Ltd, Kolkata
Bombay Gymkhana Club Ltd, Mumbai
Delhi Gymkhana Club, New Delhi
High Range Club, Kerala
India Habitat Centre, New Delhi
India International Centre, New Delhi
Jaisal Club, Rajasthan
Kodaikanal Golf Club, Tamil Nadu
Madras Gymkhana Club, Tamil Nadu
Mysore Sports Club, Mysore
Ootacamund Club, Tamil Nadu
Poona Club, Pune
Royal Bombay Yacht Club, Mumbai
Royal Calcutta Golf Club, Kolkata
Royal Calcutta Turf Club, Kolkata
Secunderabad Club, Secunderabad
Tollygunge Club Ltd, Kolkata
Willingdon Sports Club, Mumbai

Ireland
United Arts Club of Ireland, Dublin

Kenya
Mombasa Club, Mombasa
Muthaiga Club, Nairobi
Nairobi Club, Nairobi

Luxembourg
Cercle Munster, Luxembourg

Malaysia
Royal Selangor Club, Kuala Lumpur
Royal Sungei Ujong Club, Seremban

New Zealand
Auckland Club, Auckland
Canterbury Club, Christchurch
Christchurch Club, Christchurch
Dunedin Club, Dunedin
Royal New Zealand Yacht Squadron, Auckland

Nigeria
Ikoyi Club 1938, Lagos

Pakistan
Punjab Club, Lahore
Sind Club, Karachi

Philippines
Manila Club, Makati City

Portugal
Oporto Cricket and Lawn Tennis Club, Porto
Royal British Club, Estoril

The Royal Over-Seas League

Scotland
Royal Northern and University Club, Aberdeen
Western Club, Glasgow

Singapore
Singapore Cricket Club, Singapore
Tanglin Club, Singapore

South Africa
Country Club, Johannesburg (Auckland Park)
Country Club, Johannesburg (Woodmead Golf Course)
Durban Country Club, Durban
Kelvin Grove Club, Newlands

Spain
British Society, Malaga

Sri Lanka
Hill Club, Nuwara Eliya

USA
Arlington Club, Portland, Oregon
Ashford Club, Atlanta, Georgia
Cornell Club, New York
Kansas City Club, Kansas City, Missouri
Poinsett Club, Greenville, South Carolina
Standard Club, Chicago, Illinois
Union League Club of Chicago, Chicago, Illinois
Union League Club of Philadelphia, Philadelphia, Pennsylvania
University Club San Francisco, San Francisco, California

13. Annual Music Competition Prizewinners 1952–2009

Prior to 1952, the competition was known as 'The Festival of Commonwealth Youth' and was non-competitive. From 1965 until 1979, two equal first prizes were awarded to the best competitor from overseas and the best competitor from the United Kingdom.

1952	Robert Cooper	violin	Australia
1953	Geoffrey Parsons	piano	Australia
1954	Oswald Russell	piano	Jamaica
1955	Rohan de Saram	cello	Ceylon
1957	Winifred Durie	viola	Australia
1958	Audrey Cooper	piano	Jamaica
1959	Patsy Toh	piano	Hong Kong
1960	John Georgiadis	violin	UK
	Yonty Soloman	piano	South Africa
1961	Jacqueline du Pré	cello	UK
	Marjorie Biggar	contralto	Canada
1962	Ruth Little	contralto	UK
	Roy Malan	violin	South Africa
1963	John Lill	piano	UK
	Ross Pople	cello	New Zealand
1964	Sharon Mckinley	cello	Canada
	Gwennyth Annear	soprano	Australia

From 1965 until 1979, two equal first prizes were awarded to the best competitor from overseas and the best competitor from the United Kingdom.

1965	Georgetta Psaros	soprano	Australia
	Leslie Child	violin	UK
1966	Enloc Wu	piano	Hong Kong
	Hannah Francis	harp	UK
1967	David Bollard	piano	New Zealand
	Oriel Sutherland	contralto	UK
1968	Dennis Lee	piano	Malaysia
	Frank Wibaut	piano	UK
1969	Patrick Payne	contralto	New Zealand
	Penny Scott	piano	UK
1970	Geoffrey Tozer	piano	Australia
	Andrew Haigh	piano	UK
1971	Andrea Kalanj	piano	Canada
	Jan Latham Koenig	piano	UK
1972	Tessa Uys	piano	South Africa
	Marius May	cello	UK
1973	Richard Creager	tenor	New Zealand
	Anthony Smith	baritone	UK
1974	Francis Reneau	piano	Belize
	Colin Carr	cello	UK
1975	Keith Lewis	tenor	New Zealand
	Jonathan Dunsby	piano	UK
	Stewart Harling	baritone	UK
1976	Melvyn Tan	harpsichord	Singapore
	Lorraine McAslan	violin	UK
1977	Ralph de Souza	violin	India
	Aydin Onac	piano	UK
1978	Mark Walton	clarinet	New Zealand
	Suzie Meszaros	viola	UK
1979	Surendran Reddy	piano	South Africa
	Barry Douglas	piano	UK
	Jonathan Rees	violin	UK

From 1980 onwards, the first prize has been awarded to the best musicians from any country chosen from the winners of the four main solo categories (* indicates First Prize winners).

1980	Ian Graukroger	piano	Zimbabwe
	John Harle	saxophone	UK
	Peter Manning*	violin	UK
	William Shimmell	baritone	UK
1981	Wissam Boustany	flute	UK
	Jagdish Mistry	violin	India
	Jean Rigby*	mezzo-soprano	UK
	Simon Shewring	piano	UK
1982	Geoffrey Dolton	baritone	UK
	Helen Duffy	flute	UK
	Piers Lane*	piano	Australia
	Carla Maria Rodrigues	viola	UK
1983	Douglas Boyd	oboe	UK
	Susan Bullock	soprano	UK
	Christopher Marwood	cello	UK
	Jonathan Plowright*	piano	UK
1984	Lorna Anderson	soprano	UK
	Nicholas Cox*	clarinet	UK
	Gina McCormack	violin	South Africa
	Adrian Sims	piano	UK
1985	Philip Lloyd-Evans	baritone	UK
	Ieuan Jones*	harp	UK
	Anthony Marwood	violin	UK
	Jean Owen*	bassoon	UK
	Victor Sangiorgio	piano	Australia
1986	Aline Brewer	harp	UK
	Susan Chilcott*	soprano	UK
	Colin Stone	piano	UK
1987	Manuel Bagorro	piano	Zimbabwe
	Philip Levy	violin	UK
	Lucy Wakeford	harp	UK
	Janice Watson*	soprano	UK
	Michael Whight	clarinet	UK
	Read Gainsford	piano	New Zealand

The Royal Over-Seas League

1988	David Mattinson*	bass baritone	UK
	Gerard McChrystal	saxophone	UK
	Aaron Stolow	violin	UK
	Cheryl Barker	soprano	Australia
1989	Jane Evans	cor anglais	UK
	Nicola Hall*	guitar	UK
	Alvin Moisey	piano	UK
1990	William Dazeley	baritone	UK
	Rachel Gough*	bassoon	UK
	Nicholas Unwin	piano	UK
	Abigail Young	violin	UK
1991	James Brawn	piano	UK
	Janice Graham	violin	UK
	Alistair Mackie	trumpet	UK
	Adele Paxton*	soprano	UK
1992	Liam Abramson	cello	UK
	Paul Lewis	piano	UK
	Robert Plane*	clarinet	UK
	Simone Sauphanor	soprano	Trinidad & Tobago
	Neil Varley	freebass accordion	UK
1993	Sara Fulgoni	mezzo-soprano	UK
	Andrew Haveron	violin	UK
	Eryl Lloyd Williams	piano	UK
	David Preston*	freebass accordion	UK
1994	Daniel Bates*	oboe	UK
	Catryn Wyn Davies	mezzo-soprano	UK
	Priya Mitchell	violin	UK
	Roger Owens	piano	UK
1995	Annelies Chapman	soprano	New Zealand
	Sarah Markham	saxophone	UK
	Laura Samuel	violin	UK
	Ashley Wass*	piano	UK
1996	Jeanette Ager*	mezzo-soprano	UK
	Nicholas Cartledge*	flute	UK
	Viv McLean	piano	UK
	Alice Neary	cello	UK
1997	David Farmer	freebass accordion	UK
	Nicola Howard	soprano	UK
	Stuart King	clarinet	UK
	Liwei Qin*	cello	Australia

1998	Daniel Bell	violin	UK
	Gillian Keith	soprano	UK
	Fraser Tannock	trumpet	UK
	Alexander Taylor*	piano	UK
1999	Thomas Carroll	cello	UK
	Owen Dennis	oboe	UK
	Timothy Mirfin*	bass	UK
	David Quigley	piano	UK
2000	Sarah Field	saxophone	UK
	Jonathan Lemalu*	bass-baritone	New Zealand
	Benjamin Nabarro	violin	UK
	Tom Poster	piano	UK
2001	Juliette Bausor*	flute	UK
	Richard Burkhard	baritone	UK
	Danny Driver	piano	UK
	Marie Macleod	cello	UK
2002	Lucy Crowe*	soprano	UK
	Gemma Rosefield	cello	UK
	Simon Tedeschi	piano	Australia
	Eleanor Turner	harp	UK
	Sara Temple	clarinet	UK
2003	Martin Cousin*	piano	UK
	Katherine Wood	cello	UK
	Helen Vollam	trombone	UK
	Wendy-Dawn Thompson	mezzo-soprano	New Zealand
2004	Louisa Breen	piano	Australia
	Amy Dickson*	saxophone	Australia
	Anna Leese	soprano	New Zealand
	Ruth Palmer	violin	UK
2005	Nicola Eimer	piano	UK
	Timothy Orpen*	clarinet	UK
	Tamsin Waley-Cohen	violin	UK
	Elizabeth Watts	soprano	UK
2006	Mateusz Borowiak	piano	UK
	Jacques Imbrailo	baritone	South Africa
	John Myerscough*	cello	UK
	Leslie Neish	tuba	UK
2007	Daniel de Borah	piano	UK
	Jill Kemp	recorder	UK
	Pei-Sian Ng*	cello	Australia
	George von Bergen	tenor	UK

2008	Simon Ierace	keyboard
	Laura Lucas*	flute
	Victoria Simonsen	cello
	Adrian Ward	tenor
2009	Sarah Beatty	clarinet
	Yelian He	cello
	Madeleine Pierard	soprano
	Ben Schoeman*	piano

Accompanists Prize

Since 1981 the Accompanists Prize has been of equal value and status as the awards for solo performers.

1981	John Henry	UK
1982	Pamela Liddard	UK
1983	Linda Ang	Singapore
1984	Vanessa Latarche	UK
	Malcolm Martineau	UK
1985	Steven Naylor	UK
1986	Scott Mitchell	UK
1987	Rachel Franklin	UK
1988	Clare Toomer	UK
1989	Rebecca Holt	UK
1990	Elizabeth Upchurch	UK
1991	Alan Darling	UK
1992	Sophia Rahmann	UK
1993	Helen Leek	UK
1994	Julian Milford	UK
1995	Alison Proctor	UK
1996	Gretel Dowdeswell	UK
1997	Clemens Leske	Australia

1998	Stephen de Pledge	New Zealand
1999	Simon Lepper	UK
2000	Philip Moore	UK
2001	not awarded	UK
2002	Catherine Milledge	UK
2003	Huw Watkins	UK
2004	Not awarded	UK
2005	Gary Matthewman	UK
2006	Alasdair Beatson	UK
2007	Daniel Swain	UK
2008	Joseph Middleton	UK
2009	Simon Lane	UK

Ensemble Prize

Since 1980, the Ensemble Prize has been of equal status as the Gold Medal and first prize for solo performance. Since 2006 two ensemble prizes have been awarded: one for strings/keyboard and the other for wind/percussion/mixed.

1980	Trio Canello
1981	Mladi Ensemble
1982	Guildhall String Ensemble
1983	Marwood String Trio
1984	Auriol Quartet
1985	John & Katherine Lenehan Piano Duo / Lisney Piano Trio
1986	Mistry Quartet
1987	No Strings Attached
1988	Barbican Piano Trio
1989	Apollo Saxophone Quartet
1990	Techinsky Quartet
1991	Kreutzer Quartet
1992	Bone Idols
1993	not awarded
1994	Nemo Brass Quartet
1995	Leopold String Trio
1996	Micallef/Inanga Piano Duo
1997	BackBeat
1998	Newbold Piano Quartet

1999	Moore/Crawford Phillips Piano Duo	2005	Sacconi Quartet
2000	Tavec Quartet	2006	Ensemble na Mara Lancier Brass
2001	Bones Apart	2007	Cappa Quartet Zephirus
2002	Eimer Piano Trio		
2003	Bronte Quartet	2008	Brodowski Quartet Camarilla Ensemble
2004	Linos Wind Quintet Brass10	2009	Solstice Quartet St James' Quintet

In addition to the main awards listed above, the ROSL has given support and encouragement to hundreds of other gifted musicians from all over the Commonwealth through many other prizes and scholarships awarded under the umbrella of the ROSL Annual Music Competition and ROSL ARTS. A small selection of these winners is given below:

1981	Jagdish Mistry	violin	India
1986	Ian Munro	piano	Australia
	Charles Uzor	oboe	Nigeria
1987	Param Vir	composer	India
1989	Charles Uzor	oboe	Nigeria
1990	Ning Kam	violin	Singapore
1991	Ian Bostridge	tenor	UK
1992	Nathan Berg	baritone	Canada
	Carmine Lauri	violin	Malta
1993	Philip Dukes	viola	UK
	Clio Gould	violin	UK
1995	Stephen de Pledge	piano	New Zealand
	Gretchen Dunsmore	clarinet	New Zealand
	Christopher Maltman	baritone	UK
	Ashan Pillai	viola	Sri Lanka
1996	Christopher Duigan	piano	South Africa
	Glen Inanga	piano	Nigeria

1997	Karina Gauvin	soprano	Canada
	Clemens Leske	piano	Australia
	Nicholas Vines	composer	Australia
1998	Grant Doyle	baritone	Australia
	Sally Anne Russell	mezzo-soprano	Australia
1999	Catrin Finch	harp	UK
2000	Catherine Carby	mezzo-soprano	Australia
	Natalia Lomieko	violin	New Zealand
2001	Andrew Aarons	piano	Canada
	Ellen Deverall	clarinet	New Zealand
	Jared Holt	baritone	New Zealand
	Joyce Moholoagae	soprano	South Africa
	Gillian Ramm	soprano	Australia
	Bobby Chen	piano	Malaysia
2002	William Berger	baritone	South Africa
2003	Elizabeth Cooney	violin	Ireland
	Mei Yi Foo	piano	Malaysia
	Bobby Chen	piano	Malaysia
2005	James Baillieu	piano	South Africa
	Kishani Jayasinghe	soprano	Sri Lanka
2006	Brian O'Kane	cello	Ireland
	Nicholas Vines	composer	Australia
	Antipodes String Quartet	piano	New Zealand
	Michael Ierace	violin	Australia
	Victoria Mavromoustaki	violin	Cyprus
2007	Katie Stillman	piano	Canada
	Trio Scintillatum		New Zealand
	Jayson Gillham	piano	Australia
2008	Sarah Jane Brandon	soprano	South Africa

14. ROSL Annual Exhibition Prizewinners 1984–98 and Scholarship Winners 1999–2009

The ROSL Annual Exhibition, established in 1984, has provided a showcase for young artists from the UK, Commonwealth and former Commonwealth countries including Australia, The Bahamas, Bangladesh, Barbados, Belize, Canada, Cyprus, Ghana, Grenada, Hong Kong, India, Ireland, Jamaica, Kenya, Malaysia, Malta, Mauritius, New Zealand, Nigeria, Pakistan, Singapore, South Africa, Sri Lanka, Tanzania, Trinidad and Tobago, Uganda and the UK (* indicates First Prize winners).

1984

Christopher Cook	UK	Trevor Landell	UK
Julie Held*	UK	Shanti Panchal	India
Miles Hunter	Canada	Elizabeth Willis	UK
Maggie James	UK		

1985

Michael Croft	UK	William Macilraith	UK
Valerie Dunant	UK	Neil Macpherson*	UK
Amanda Faulkner	UK	Gerard Morris	UK
Yvonne Forward	UK	Emma McClure	UK
Wendy Hodge	Canada		

1986

Iona Campbell-Gray	UK	Julie Held	UK
Philip Davies*	UK	Emma McClure	UK
Jason Gibilaro	UK	John Skinner	UK

1987

Sonia Boyce*	UK		Judy Inglis	UK
Nicholas Fredman	UK		Stephen Rose	UK
Alexander Guy	UK		Colin Smith*	UK
Roderick Henriques	UK		Patricia Wright	UK

1988

Patricia Gardner	UK		Sally Moore	UK
Stephen Goddard	UK		Jake Tilson*	UK
Leslie Hakim-Dowek*	UK			

1989

Stacy Billups	UK		Julian Hyam	UK
Martin Churchill	UK		Robin Mason*	UK
Rory Donaldson	UK		Tara Sabharwal	India
Paul Furneaux	UK			

1990

Martin Churchill	UK		Susan Ryland	UK
Christopher Cook	UK		Rebecca Salter	UK
Lynn Dennison	UK		Tai-Shan Schierenberg*	UK
Nicholas Romeril	UK			

1991

Susan Adams	UK		Mark Burrell	UK
Lesley Banks	UK		Moyra Derby	UK
Tracy Beckerley	UK		Anne Desmet	UK
Simon Brewster	UK		Christopher Nurse*	UK

The Royal Over-Seas League

1992

Murshida Arzu Alpana	Bangladesh	Gayle Nelson	UK
Andrew Bick	UK	Melissa Scott-Miller	UK
Shirley Chubb	UK	Judith Weil	UK
Lee Wing Keung	Hong Kong	Kim Williams*	UK
Atta Kwami	Ghana		

1993

Ben Cook	UK	Joseph Mathew	India
Elysia Dywan	Canada	Michael John Shaw	UK
Joe Fan*	UK	Jane Walker	UK
Nigel Jensen	UK	Charles Williams	UK
Mark Masters	Canada	Lisa Wright	UK

1994

Lucy Bentley	UK	Patrick Mazola	Kenya
Ma Choi	Hong Kong	Arabella Ross	UK
Jonathan Cole	UK	Paul Ryan	UK
Shelly Goldsmith	UK	Stephanie Sampson	UK
Mohd Azhar Abd Manan*	Malaysia	Balakrishnan Sreegopan	India

1995

Pindaro Cabrera	Canada	Sophie Herxheimer	UK
Martin Constable	UK	Caroline List*	UK
Michael Cubey	New Zealand	Sally Meyer	UK
		Stuart Robertson	UK
Joan Dymianiw	Canada	Charles Williams	UK

1996

Marika Borlase	Australia	Joanne Hodgen	UK
Alan Brooks*	UK	Bharti Kher	UK
Jenny Dolezel	New Zealand	Sista Pratesi	UK
		Aimie Reeves	UK
Sarah Durcan	Ireland	Amrit Singh	UK

1997

Guy Buckles	UK	Nigel Mullins*	South Africa
Helen Flockhart	UK	Pradeep Sukumaran	India
Christopher		Renny Tait	UK
Gilvan-Cartwright	UK	Robert White	UK
Vincent Graves-Aggrey	Ghana	Charles Williams	UK

1998

Isobel Brigham	UK	Grace O'Connor	Ireland
Andrew Cranston*	UK	Joe Painter	UK
John Dargan	UK	Philip Parham	UK
Derek McGuire	UK	MTPV Satyanarayana	India
Todd Narbey	New Zealand		

Visual Arts Travel Scholarships:

Since 1999 ROSL ARTS has offered five Visual Arts Travel Scholarships annually. These scholarships enable selected artists to make a study visit to or undertake a residency in a Commonwealth country other than their country of origin. In the year following their scholarship study visit or residency the scholars are brought together for a group exhibition in London.

1999	Pindaro Cabrera	Canada
	Todd Narbey	Canada
	Ming Wong	Singapore
2000	Matthew Burrows	UK
	Fiona Couldridge	South Africa
	Mzukesi Dyaloyi	South Africa
	Nahid Niazi	Bangladesh
	Savandhary Vongpoothorn	Australia
2001	Joseph Cartoon	Kenya
	Bella Easton	UK
	Belinda Harrow	Canada/New Zealand
	John Lai	Malaysia
	Heather Straka	New Zealand

2002	Sudath Abeysekera	Sri Lanka
	Kwadwo Ani	Ghana
	Deborah Bowness	UK
	Christine Morrow	Australia
	Ebony Patterson	Jamaica
2003	Matt Couper	New Zealand
	Jason Hicks	New Zealand
	Kwok Cheun Lee	Hong Kong
	J. Henry Mujunga	Uganda
	Ruth Uglow	UK
2004	Jemima Burrill	UK
	Sohan Ariel Hayes	Australia
	Ally Nyomwa	Tanzania
	Shanti Persaud	Jamaica
	Ratheesh Thankamma	India
2005	Daisy Jackson	New Zealand
	Ali Kazim	Pakistan
	Ryan Mosley	UK
	Justin Partyka	UK
	Nicholas Twist	New Zealand
2006	Aimee Lax	UK
	Joseph Mattew	India
	Paul Ryan	UK
	Allyson Reynolds	Australia
	Francois Simard	Canada
2007	Jacob Carter	UK
	Joanna Langford	New Zealand
	Christina Papakyriakou	Cyprus
	Lauren Porter	UK
	Jeremy Sharma	Singapore
2008	Melanie Fitzmaurice	Australia
	Liliane Nabulime	Uganda
	Kazi Sahid	Bangladesh
	Michele Fletcher	Canada
2009	Anikpe Ebene	Nigeria
	Chan Kok Hooi	Malaysia
	Keegan Simon	Trinidad and Tobago
	Todd Stratton	Australia

Notes

Introduction

1   Robert Browning, 'Andrea del Sarto', 1855.

I – Evelyn Wrench and the Founding of the Royal Over-Seas League

1   The *Boy's Own Paper* was a collection of stories and articles aimed at young and teenage boys. It was published by various publishers including the Religious Tract Society, Lutterworth Press, Purnell and Sons and BPC Publishing between the years 1879 and 1967. For more information see the Wikipedia entry at *http://en.wikipedia.org/wiki/ Boy%27s_Own*.

2   Richard Jebb, *Colonial Nationalism* (London: Edward Arnold, 1905); Norman Angell, *The Great Illusion* (New York and London: G.P. Putnam's Sons, 1913), developed from his 1909 pamphlet *Europe's Optical Illusion*.

3   In the 1840s Henry Mayhew observed, documented and described the state of working people in London for a series of articles in the *Morning Chronicle* newspaper. These were later compiled into *London Labour and the London Poor*, with three volumes published in 1851 and a further book in the series was published in 1861. More recent editions were published by Dover Publications in 1968 (Vols 1–3) and 1983 (Vol. 4).

4   In John Evelyn Wrench, *Uphill* (London: Ivor Nicholson and Watson, 1934), pp.158–62.

5   Ibid., p.242.

6   See n.2.

7   The award Companion of the Order of St Michael and St George.

8   From a letter of sympathy after the death of Sir Evelyn Wrench to the then Director General, Philip Crawshaw.

9 Quotation in the Courtyard of Dartmouth House, the English-Speaking Union Headquarters.

II – Development of the League

1 John Evelyn Wrench, *Immortal Years* (London: Hutchinson and Co., 1945).

2 The award of Knight Commander of the Order of St Michael and St George.

3 Sir Jocelyn Lucas, from pamphlet 'The Allies Welcome Committee 1940–1950', ROSL archives, London.

IV – Communications

1 From 'The Story of the Over-Seas League', an in-house article written '28 years after its inception' by Sir Evelyn Wrench.

2 From 'Over-Seas League in the Year of the Coronation of His Majesty King George VI' (in-house publication, 1937).

3 Many thanks to the family of Philip Noakes who hold these records and have given permission for use of the quotations from his diaries and private letters in this book.

V – The Branches, Honorary Corresponding Secretaries and Reciprocal Clubs

1 Over Seas League Annual Report, 1926.

VI – Over-Seas House, London and Edinburgh, Architecture and History

1 From an article by Sir Evelyn Wrench in 1937 to mark the completion of the Westminster Wing.

2 Ibid.

3 *The Dunciad* by Alexander Pope was first published anonymously in 1728.

4 *The Daily Advertiser*, April 1731.

5 From 'Over-Seas House, London, Past and Present', (London: ROSL), p.5, an in-house booklet giving a history of the ROSL and Over-Seas House

6   For all direct quotations and terms ascribed to Lady Diana Cooper in this section see Chapter 1 of Diana Cooper, *The Rainbow Comes and Goes* (London: Rupert Hart-Davis, 1958).

VIII – The League Today

1   Letter to the author, 28 July 2008.

2   Sir Evelyn Wrench, quoted in Michael Wynne-Parker, *Bridge Over Troubled Water* (Cambridge: Granta Editions, 1996), p.103.

3   From ESU promotional brochure.

4   In conversation with PR Director Margaret Adnan-Vallence in Namibia, as reported to the author.

5   In conversation with PR Director Margaret Adnan-Vallence in Namibia, cited in ROSL Annual Report 2007.

Index

Page references in italics refer to illustrations.

The colour illustrations between pages 96 and 97 are shown as e.g. col 2*, where the 2 refers to the numbering of these illustrations.